# ANTHROPOLOGY OF DEVELOPMENT

# ANTHROPOLOGY OF DEVELOPMENT

## Demystifications and Relevance

*By*

**Dr. Jaganath Pathy**

GYAN

Anthropology of Development


ISBN : 978-81-212-0081-3



First Published 1987, reprint 2013 in India by
Gyan Publishing House
23, Main Ansari Road, Daryaganj,
New Delhi - 110002
Phones : 23282060, 23261060
Fax : (011) 23285914
E-mail: books@gyanbooks.com
website: gyanbooks.com

*Printed at* : Sagar Color Scan, New Delhi.

# CONTENTS

# 1

# IMPERIALISM, ANTHROPOLOGY AND THE THIRD WORLD

ANTHROPOLOGY, like all other social sciences, is historically and socially conditioned. It originated in the colonial milieu to meet primarily the administrative problems which arose in the process of expansion and consolidation of colonialism. Therefore, for a long time, it continued to reflect the interests of the colonial empires. With the rise of national movements, colonialism got disintegrated and decayed; but ironically, most of the politically independent countries came to be dominated by the United States.

Simultaneously, however, the trend for struggles to achieve liberation from all sorts of social exploitations, specially imperialist exploitation, has been set in motion in the third world. In this changing situation imperialism is involved not only in expropriating surplus but also during the people with suitable policies and propaganda. Anthropology reacted favourably to the changing situation, and in turn, procured patronage of the imperialist agencies and their allies in the third world. Accordingly anthropology of development, as it is practised today, is largely, if not wholly, a reflection of the above design. This paper seeks to elaborate the connections.

## ANTHROPOLOGY AND COLONIALISM

Anthropology as a distinct discipline emerged and flourished along with the expansion of colonial imperium. The *raison d'etre* for anthropology was to facilitate colonial administration by discovering ways of governing and controlling the colonised people (Owusu. 1975 : Introduction). The subject became an aid and comfort to the colonial powers (Boissevain, 1974) Anthropologists parti ipated in the power and privileges of the dominant groups (Memmi, 1967 : 17) and justified the actions of the colonial governments on the ground that the native people had no knowledge of what was good for themselves : hence the colonial powers in their mission to civilise the 'savage' had to be assisted in all possible ways. According to Evans-Pritchard. "if it is the policy of a colonial government to administer a people through their chiefs it is useful to know who are the chiefs and what are their functions and authority and privileges and obligations Also, if it is intended to administer a people according to their own laws and customs one has first to discover what those are" (1951 : 109-110). Likewise, Firth (1956 : Chapter VII) acknowledges the role of anthropologists within the limits of the colonial governments settled policy.

In a sense. colonialism was the normal world for the anthropologists (Gough. 1968). An anthropologist wrote : "Colonisation has always required the existence of the need for dependence. Not all peoples can be colonised : only those who experience this need" (Mannoni 1956 : 85) Thus in a stroke, the piratical plunder of the third world resources from 16th to 19th century, which deformed and sometimes destroyed thriving civilisations while consistently augmenting the affluence and opulence of Europe is rationalised. "What Man's Burden" was propagated in the face of deportations, forced labour, slavery and massacres leaning to a high rate of extinction of the local population. The colonised people starved in building capitalism in the West. The subversion of traditional customs and mutilation of the native languages and cultures by colonialism was safely attended within the circle of Malinowski's insinuation (1961: 158-9) rather than through expropriation and exploitation. Levi-Strauss rightly remarked: "Anthropology . . . is the outcome of a historical process which has made the large part of mankind subservient to the other and during which millions of human beings have had their resources plundered and their institutions and beliefs destroyed, whilst they themselves were ruthlessly killed, thrown into bondage, and contaminated by diseases they were unable to resist" (1966 : 158-59).

Anthropological research was carried out in Asia and Africa under the protective umbrella of the colonial authorities. Colonised people were treated as mere objects of study (Levi-Strauss, 1966 : 126): and for an object equivalent of white rat in a laboratory used for 'advancement of science', one does not require to have any serious obligations (Memmi, 1967 : 86). These studies assisted the colonialists in the implementation of their policies. The type of esoteric interests of anthropologists and their exaggeration of the segmentary and pluralistic foci of the colonised societies through the details of ethnic and religious groups conveyed disunity among the people and contributed to the 'divide and rule' policy of the colonial regimes.

In the whole of nineteenth century anthropology revolved around the notion that the culture of the Anglo-Saxon world represented the ideal and peak of civilisation and human development (Mair, 1963). and acquainted the colonial administrators with the diversity of customs in different segments of the population (Dube, 1962 : 237-38). The colonised people were called primitive, apathetic and static. The myth of the 'noble and contended savage' was spread all over the colonised world. There was also stress on their moral inferiority which helped to maintain the *status quo* of colonialism (Diamond, 1971 : 172). This was the time when colonialism was expanding.

But with the development of nationalist movements in the colonised world, functional and structural-functional schools were brought into the anthropological investigations. Functionalists in their desire to establish an administration with minimal friction studied European contacts with indigenous cultures. The romantic idealisation of indigenous culture and institutions portrayed a happy society, and the commitment to preserve the institutions and cultures through the policy of 'indirect rule' were squarely hostile to change. The paternalistic and hypocritical notion of cultural determinism was very much in the air. Mair makes the point explicit in African context: "We all made ourselves the defenders of African custom against its critics, and against policies aimed at radical change... We used to say that people should learn from the industrial revolution in Europe and so spare Africa its worst horrors" (1965 : 439-40).

Whatever changes occurred in anthropology, within the span of colonial period, was structurally determined by the then prevailing socio-historical forces. Maquet writes : "Most anthropological studies were conservative : first, in that Africans were described as so different from 'civilised' peoples and so 'savage' just at the time that Europe needed to justify colonial expansion; and second, in that later on, the value of the traditional cultures was magnified when it was useful for the colonial powers to ally themselves with the more traditional forces against the progressive Africans. We do not believe that those parallels are mere coincidences" (1964 : 50).

In addition to this rationalising role, the colonial anthropologists appeared in operational roles in war time. They compiled ethnographic records which passed often as "detailed intelligence reports" (Forde, 1953 : 845). The misuse of anthropology and the deplorable role of anthropologists as spies during World War I was publicly denounced by Boas (1919 : 797). During the Second World War, anthropologists were in great demand to analyse the cultures of different people for formulation of policies in the occupied areas and to prepare manuals for troops. During that war Ruth Benedict was asked to compile a report on Japanese collective attitudes. Besides, Evans-Pritchard led Anuak guerillas, in Southern Sudan (Gluckman, 1965: 166, note 1), and Leach had "engaged" in raising a force of Kachin irregulars" in Burma (1964: 311). Many anthropologists like Evan-Pritchard, Nadel and Audrey Richards acted as colonial administrators in Africa during the war. It is a small wonder, then, that following the disintegration of the colonial system, there has been an acrimonious debate over the relationship between anthropology and colonialism (Asad, 1975).

## ANTHROPOLOGY AND IMPERIALISM

After the Second World War, the United States emerged as the most powerful country in the world. It became the protector, defender and guardian of Western imperialism. In order to enhance imperialist aggression, increase investment and accumulate profits for its corporations, it required information about the ex-colonial countries of Asia, Africa and Latin America. Consequently, enormous funds are spent for collection of data. Among others, anthropologists have responded favourably to provide expertise for the purpose (Saberwal, 1970).

Since the beginning of the 1950s various corporate trustees like Carnegie, Ford, Lee, Rand, Rockfeller and the Smithsonian Foundations; a number of institutions like Hudson Institute, International Development Research Centre (Canada), Population Council (New York); a number of Universities like Michigan State, Chicago and California (with its "language and area study programmes"); and the American government through its National Science Foundation, AID, World Bank, IMF, Advance Research Projects Agency of the Department of Defence, including CIA have been financing research projects in third world countries. Invariably, these agencies support such projects which are in conformity with the current socio-cultural values and are intimately linked with the interest of the Establishment. Anthropologists through their researches help these agencies by providing varied techniques of indoctrination to ensure social conformity and political passivity. In fact, the attempt is primarily to divert attention from the fundamental contradictions in society and bring order to the prevailing turbulent situation by propagating the idea that development is possible by adopting the modern imported or foreign collaborated technology, and suggest various 'pacifying' programmes in that regard (Tullis, 1973 : 7).

The most bewildering thing, however, is the dissemination of propaganda literature in glossy academic jackets (Pathy, 1976). The anthropological syllabi in the universities in the third world are packed with conservative concepts and reactionary theories.

Consensus among all the members of a society is tactically presumed while change is solely ascribed to external factors. The prescribed text-books, mostly originating from the United States, are supplied at low cost or distributed freely through official and semi-official information agencies.

Through all these means, imperialism has reaped its harvest. It has convinced most of the 'national' governments to accept its guidance in planning; turned third world anthropologists to obedient followers: got required information for more and more expropriation of third world resources without being challenged: popularised propaganda as science and transformed many third world anthropologists into apostles of conservation. In fact, anthropology is an epiphenomenon of colonialism and its present existence is largely due to neo-colonialism. There is the same ultimate stultifying mystique of maintenance and conservation of order.

According to a study commissioned by the American Anthropological, Association, "Anthropologists ...have been full or part time employees of the United States intelligence agencies including the CIA especially, either directly or through grants from certain foundations with questionable sources of income, or as employees of private research organisations . . ." (Nelson, 1966). It is also found that not only the social scientists have intimate relationship individually with the Pentagon and intelligence wings of the United States (Horowitz, 1968), but many professional organisations too are under the general influence of CIA (Stern, 1967). Many well-known anthropologists have confidentially provided politically convenient information and have engaged in 'counter-insurgency' projects in third world countries. Notable among these have been the project Agile in Thailand (Braestrued, 1967), the Latin American Counter Insurgency Research, Camelot, sponsored and financed by the United States Army and involving in subjects of greater sensitivity. (Horowitz, 1965 : Lowe, 1966), the role of Michigan State University in Vietnam and its relationship with the CIA (Horowitz, 1966 : Hinkle, 1966).

It is not surprising therefore, that anthropology in Asia and Africa are alien to the local people, and has been persistently denounced for its past colonial affiliation and its present imperialist connections.

## ANTHROPOLOGY OF DEVELOPMENT

Anthropology of development has emerged as a kind of community development and social work for the third world, which is expected to develop gradually in a cumulative way by participating in Western science, technology, education and culture. The most attractive problem has been to evolve a strategy to minimise psychological as well as economic dislocations, resulting from industrialisation.

Applied anthropological studies are conducted at microlevel situations within the framework of structural functionalism. Change is analysed with the help of conservative concepts like cultural contact, acculturation, folk-urban continuum, bridge action, Westernisation, urbanisation, modernisation, etc. The divisions of people into inferiors and superiors are sanctified through the theories of social darwinism and cultural relativism. The obstacles to development are cleverly located in ecology, ideology, lethargy, lack of capital, expertise, traditional practices and ideas and values.

In short, being totally insensitive to class and national exploitations, the developmental anthropologists forward the thesis that without the continuing diffusion of capital, technology and institutions from the West, the third world cannot develop (Frank, 1971 : 27). This thesis ultimately, eulogises imperialist policies of unequal trade, arms, sale, and ideological propaganda.

Besides anthropology of development holds that change should be gradual; that rapid or massive structural transformations should be avoided, as they are inherently harmful. Social revolutions are not the only means for social change and economic advance while they dislocate and create confusion in the contended societies (Onwuachi and Wolfe, 1966). In addition, change is considered external, and the causes of social change are thought to be multiple which can be properly studied within a small and manageable community. Multiple factoral approach bisasically a bourgeois idea to counter the Marxian premise. And the methodological insistence on small communities as self-contained entities precludes the study of role of colonialism and imperialism (Magubane, 1971).

We have already noted that applied anthropology lacks a sound theory of social change and is most obviously involved in the perpetuation of neo-colonial system (Foster, 1969 : 194-96). This can be further seen by a review of the major theories of development in anthropology like enculturation, community development and modernisation.

*Enculturation :* There is considerable body of literature dealing with the problems of acculturation and social change. The attention is focused on the behaviour and value systems of the accultured people, as if they exercised free choice. Universally, the case is that whenever two cultures at different levels of technological development meet, there is resistance and through violence the weaker yield to the stronger, after profound modifications. The indigenous people are always forcibly reconciled to the *fait accompli.*

Most studies are infused with such ethnocentrism without a recognition of the fact that the people have been robbed of their culture and identity. Scholars of enculturation, however, consider this as natural. The studies are presented without recognising the fires which blaze underneath the encultured' societies. They tend to obscure the imperial, ethnic and class structure of society and play down the monopoly of powers. The colonialism and imperialism have been surreptitiously using these works to mask their real mission of subverting the aspirations and struggles of the oppressed people of the third world—but behind a veneer of academic professionalism.

*Community Development :* During the 1950s, several American anthropologists and foundations, notably the Ford Foundation, spread the message of community development to the third world governments (Srinivas and Panini, 1973: 199). The programme was visualised as the most efficient method for rural transformation.

The striking assumptions of the programme are that it should involve all the households of village community irrespective of class, caste, creed or sex; and that the planning and execution should be based on cultural values, norms and traditions of the people. The first assumption, without acknowledging the inherited disparities in the social structure, was instrumental in widening the already existing divisions among the various agrarian classes. It is utopian to think that there would be more or less equal distribution of benefits in the face of dominant landlords and usurers. The second assumption impressed that conflicts can be avoided in the process of social change.

The crux of the programme, however, was to facilitate adoptation of Western technologies and justify foreign 'aid'; that is, to enable international corporation to reap profits without a challenge from the people. Comprador leaderships did accept the programme uncritically, and before the futility of the programme was realised, the imperialist anthropologists and other social scientists had discovered the theories of modernisation.

*Modernisation :* In the 1960s the study of development in third world countries was dominated by the theories of modernisation—a derivative of structural functionalism. It is characterised by the neglect of history, internal and external structure of domination and dependence, and swayed by anti-communism and ethnocentrism. It does not question the legitimacy of the prevailing power structures.

The implicit assumption of modernisation are that (*i*) backwardness is primarily the function of cultural and institutional elements of underdeveloped countries; (*ii*) the societies of the West, particularly North America, are the ideal cases of modernised social structures, and the traditional societies should seek to emulate this model; (*iii*) the benefits achieved by a state in terms of GNP, per capita income, etc. through the Western help would help the general mass simultaneously; and, (*iv*) modernisation of traditional societies can be attained without destroying or modifying the structure.

Obviously, the mechanical equation between the essence of

modernisation and Westernisation is left undisturbed, while the former is considered as symbolic to the forces of progress. Capitalism is indirectly suggested as desirable for the third world. This ignores the colonial past and the present domination of advanced industrial countries on the underdeveloped world. Secondly, the fact that by eliminating private ownership in the means of production, vast areas of the world are developing along the socialist lines is completely ignored in the voluminous works of Western scholars and their followers in third world countries. Thirdly, to expropriate through unequal trade, the West has prescribed the necessity of outside 'help' without recognition of the concrete reality that the third world can develop remarkably with negligible outside assistance if only it can fight against imperialism and local ruling classes and, thereby, divert the resources for production purposes. Fourthly, the contrast between capitalism and socialism as stages of development or alternative forms within industrial society is either obscured or deliberately excluded. Fifthly, the changes going on in the West tend to be neglected while, changes expected in the third world are presumed to appear in gradual-cumulative process through fluctuations. Besides, there is no distinction made between revolutionary and non-revolutionary changes in developmental process.

As a result of the acceptance of this irrelevant and outrageously reactionary policy, there has been massive inflow of finance capital, technology and knowhow. A large part of the surplus went out of the third world countries and the educated parasitical groups. In consequence, the proportion of people below poverty line grew rapidly. In the name of modernisation, atrocities were (and are) committed on the peasant and working classes, whenever they raised their just demands. Unemployment and underemployment grew phenomenally. Continual dependence on the imperialist countries for a vast array of production goods and other commodities restrained the inherent potential for development, while the foreign 'aid' compelled the third world countries to toe the lines of imperialism. Neo-colonialism could mature in the framework.

In sum, the various anthropological theories of development

are metaphysical, isolationist, anti-dialectical and anti-historical. They do not enumerate the inner contradictions of a system and its revolutionary leaps. Relative permanence and stability of the social system is absolutised, ruling out the possibility of discovering the essence of social relationships. Thus development as it is used in anthropology is a perfect justification for pillage.

## ANTHROPOLOGY AND UNDERDEVELOPMENT

With all these developmental policies and foreign 'aid', the third world instead of developing is "slipping backwards" (Worsley, 1970: 324) and was estimated to contain (in 1975) approximately 750 million poverty stricken people (World Bank, 1975 : 120-24).

The backwardness of the third world is not due to cultural reasons, it is the indirect result of the historical relationship between the third world and the Western world. It is the result of the historical process of capitalist development in the West over the last four centuries (Brett, 1973). The perpetuation of this underdevelopment has been due to imperialist domination of the political economy of these countries (Arrighi and Saul, 1973; Fanon, 1966: 119-63). Thus underdevelopment of the third world can be meaningfully analysed only by studying its relations to colonialism and imperialism which simultaneously destroyed and preserved precapitalist modes of production [Mao, 1975 (3); Chattopadhyay, 1972; and Resnick, 1973].

By the outbreak of First Word War, colonies and dependencies accounted for roughly two-thirds of the world's territory and 60 per cent of its population (Brutents, 1972: 7). Britain alone had 55 colonies with a population of 400 million. Colonialism deliberately supported and sought to perpetuate precapitalist relations and did everything to prevent the development of local industries, with the exception of mining, plantation and certain subsidary industries.

With the disintegration of colonialism, imperialism has been using the third world as a market for the products of its own industry, and thereby inhibiting the indigenous growth. In addition, it procures primary goods from its 'dependent territory' and exploits local natural resources and labour. Over time, there has been a rapid growth in the overseas operation of US corporations. In 1950, their investment was $10,000 million which by 1971 had increased to $86,000 million (Chomsky, 1973: 21). In between 1971 and 1973, about $ 8788.9 million outflowed from the third world as profit (Clairmonte, 1975). In 1975, the deficit in the balance of payment in the third world had reached an unprecedented total of $45,000 million and the external debt had risen to $215,000 million. Dependent and disarticulated development is thus reinforced by a regime of multinational corporations.

Backwardness of the third world being the product of the colonial and neo-colonial exploitation and obsolete social relations at home, the crucial problem before the third world is to fight against imperialism and its lackeys.

Development is the struggle of opposites, governed by and subordinated to the continuous struggle of the producers to dominate over their product and the conditions of production. It does not proceed harmoniously or mechanically in a step by step way. Effective resistance to imperialism, history informs us, is rarely accomplished without decisive struggles of the oppressed people. It is also disastrous to assume that development of the third world can take place without bringing about radical structural transformations. "The basic question before Asian countries today . . . is one of dismantling the citadels of power and vested interests that are obstacles to their growth. The entrenched economic interests that create social and political privilege need to be attacked first" (Dube, 1976 : 85). The third world can develop only through social revolution, for that only can break the enclave of underdevelopment (Wertheim, 1974).

Anthropological ideology, being determined by colonialism in the past and neo-colonialism in recent days, has taken up those facts as given. These have to be changed. The most important and challenging role the progressive anthropologists can play is to demystify and expose, historically and contextually, what has been done in the name of anthropology. This is a formidable task.

In order to locate the problem in proper perspective, the progressive anthropologists need to approach large scale regional, national and international phenomena instead of a community, traditional to the discipline. Besides, finding a problem is inadequate unless the scholar participates in solving that. As Mao rightly argued, the underlying principle of knowledge is : "If you want to know a certain thing or a certain class of things directly, you must personally participate in the practical struggle to change that thing or class of things, for only thus can you come into contact with them as phenomena, only through your personal participation in the practical struggle to change reality can you uncover the essence of that thing or class of things and comprehend them" (1975 : 299-300).

In the pursuit, the anthropologists should shed their value-neutrality and stop opposing large scale changes. The need is to transform anthropology from being an instrument of domination of the oppressors to becoming an instrument of liberation of the oppressed.

## *REFERENCES*

Arrighi, Giovanni, and John S. Saul (1973): "Essays on the Political Economy of Africa", Monthly Review Press, New York.

Asad, Talal (Ed) (1975): "Anthropology and the Colonial Encounter", Ithaca Press, London.

Boas, Frantz (1919): 'Scientists as Spies', *Nation*, 109, 797.

Boissevian, Jeremy (1974): "Friend of Friends: Networks, Manipulators and Coalitions", St. Martin's Press, New York.

Bonfil, Batalla, Guillermo (1966): 'Conservative Thought in Anthropology: A Critique', *Human Organisation*, Volume 25, pp. 89-92.

Braestrued, Peter (1967): 'Researchers Aid and Thai Rebel Fight: US Defence Unit develops anti-guerilla devices', *New York Times*, March 20.

Brett, E. A. (1973): "Colonialism and Underdevelopment in East Africa 1919-1939", Heinemann, London.

Brutents, K. (1972): "A Historical View of Neocolonialism", Novosti Press Agency, Moscow.

Chattopadhyaya, Paresh (1972): 'The Mode of Production in Indian Agriculture', *Economic and Political Weekly*, December 30.

Chomsky, Noam (1973): 'Scholarship and Ideology: American Historians as 'Experts in Legitimation', *Social Scientist*, Volume 1, Number 7.

Clairmonte, Frederick F. (1975): 'Dynamics of International Exploitation', *Economic and Political Weekly*, August 9.

Diamond, Stanley (1971): 'Man and Superman', *Partisan Review*, Volume 2, pp. 167-82.

Dube, S. C. (1962): 'Social Anthropology in India', in "Indian Anthropology: Essays in Memory of D. N. Majumdar", Edited by T. N. Madan and Gopal Saran, Asia Publishing House, Bombay.

——(1976): 'Social and Cultural Factors in Development', in "Asian Rethinking of Development", edited by Yogesh Atal and Ralph Pieris, Abinav Publications, New Delhi.

Evans-Pritchard. E. E. (1951): "Social Anthropology", London.

Fanon. Frantz (1966): "The Wretched of the Earth", Grove Press, New York.

Firth, Raymond (1956): "Human Types", London.

Forde. C D. (1953): 'Applied Anthropology in Government: British Africa' in "Anthropology Today" edited by A. L. Kroeber, University of Chicago Press. Chicago.

Foster, George (1969): "Applied Anthropology", Little Brown, Boston.

Frank Andre G. (1971): "The Sociology of Development and the Underdevelopment of Sociology", Pluto Press, London.

Gluckman. Max (1965): "Politics, Law and Ritual in Tribal Society' Aldine. Chicago.

Gough, Katharine (1968): 'Anthropology: Child of Imperialism', *Monthly Review*. Volume 19, Number 11.

Binkle. Warren (1966): 'MSU: The University On the Make', *Ramparts*. Volume 4, Number 12.

Horowitz, Irving Lewis (1965): 'The Life and Death of Project Camelot', *Trans-Action*, Volume 3.

——(1966): 'Michigan State and the CIA: A Dilemma for Social Science', *Bulletin of the Atomic Scientists.* Volume 22, Number 7.

——(1968): 'Social Science Yogis and Military Commissars: An Analysis of the Contents and Implications of a Confidential Report of How Social Science Research Can Benefit the Defence Department', *Trans-Action*, May.

Leach, E. R. (1964): "Political Systems of Highland Burma', Beacon Press, Boston.

Levi-Strauss, Claude (1966): 'Anthropology : Its Achievements and Future' *Current Anthropology*, Volume 7.

Lowe, George E (1966): 'The Camelot Affair', *Bulletin of the Atomic Scientists*, Volume 22, Number 5.

Magubane, Bernard (1971): 'A Critical Look at Indices Used in the Study of Social Change in Colonial Africa ', *Current Anthropology*, Volume 12.

Mair, Lucy (1963) : "New Nations" Weidenfeld and Nicholson, London.

——(1965): "Tradition and Modernity in the New Africa', *Transactions of the New York Academy of Sciences*, Volume 27.

Malinowski, Bronislaw (1961): "Argonauts of the Western Pacific", Dutton, New York.

Mannoni, O. (1956): "Prospero and Caliban. The Psychology of Colonisation", Methuen, London.

Mao Tse-tung (1975): "Selected Works", Foreign Languages Press, Peking.

Maquet, Jacques (1964): 'Objectivity in Anthropology', *Current Anthropology*, Volume 5.

Memmi, Albert (1967): "The Coloniser and the Colonised", Beacon Press, Boston.

Nelson, Bryce (1966): 'Anthropologists' Debate: Concern Over Future of Foreign Research', *Science*, Volume 159.

Onwuachi, P. Chikwe, and Wolfe Alvin W. (1966): "The Place of Anthropology in the Future of Africa", *Human Organisation*, Volume 25.

Owusu, Maxwell (*ed*) (1975): "Colonialism and Change", Mouton, Hague.

Pathy, Jaganath (1976): 'Underdevelopment of Indian Sociology', *Social Scientist*, Volume 4, Number 11.

Resnick, S. A. (1973): 'The Second Path to Capitalism', *Journal of Contempor ıry Asia*, Volume 3, Number 20.

Saberwal, Satish (1970): 'International Social Science: Some Political Aspects', *Economic and Political Weekly*, July 4.

Srinivas, M. N. and Panini M. N. (1973): 'Development of Sociology and Social Anthropology in India', *Sociological Bulletin*, Volume 22, Number 20.

Stern, Sol (1976): 'NSA and the CIA: A Short Account of International Student Politics and the Cold War', *Ramparts*, Volume 5, Number 9.

Tullis, F. L. A. (1973):"Politics and Social Change in Third World Countries", John Wiley, New York.

Wertheim, W. F. (1974): "The Rising Waves of Emancipation from Counterpoint Towards Revolution" in "Sociology and Development", edited by Kadt and Williams, Tavistock, London.

World Bank (1975): "The Assault on World Poverty Problems of Rural Development Education and Health".

Worsely, Peter (1970): "The Third World", University of Chicago Press, Chicago.

# 2

# CROSS-CULTURAL INEQUALITY : THE ANTHROPOLOGICAL CONCERN

INEQUALITY has always attracted the attention of social theorists and philosophers. Ancient and medieval thinkers justified social disparities in terms of their naturalness. Aristotle contended that men are by nature inequal in rank. And thus 'there are *by nature* freemen and slaves, and that servitude is agreeable and just. . . . Equally the relation of the male to the female *by nature* such that one is superior and the other inferior, one dominates and other is dominated. . .' (Aristotle. 1959). Being a natural phenomenon inequality is inevitable and immutable.[1] The Aristotelian theory of some races destined to be the masters while others capable of nothing provided the rationale and apologia for the rape and despoliation of the Third World. Anyway, it was only after the American and French revolutions that inequality became a subject for scientific investigation and received various degrees of reprobation. Rousseau, a rebel against inequality, argued that in the 'state of nature' there was complete equality of all. Inequality emerged due to man's divorce from the 'state of nature'— the original sin !

1. Continuity of this explanation to inequality can be discerned not only at the abstract theoretical level but also in the concrete cultural discourses of the dominated peoples. At the risk of digression, it is tempting to note that one of the most common symbols used by the Oriyas (of Orissa, India) to justify socio-cultural inequality is to show that the fingers of a hand are by nature unequal. To what extent this sort of logic is imposed involuntarily on the majority is, of course, another matter.

Though he distinguished two kinds of inequalities, viz., the natural or physical inequality 'established by nature, and consists in a difference of age, health, bodily strength and the qualities of mind or the soul' and the other, 'moral or political inequality established by the consent of men' (1912 : 160), he preferred to ignore the former. Like him, Ferguson (1767), Millar (1771) and others assumed a natural state of inequality, and regarded property as chief source in creating inequality. Their works implied that since society, the creator of inequality, is subject to change, the inequality will also ultimately and inevitably change. It needs to be stressed here that this ideal of equality originated with the advent of capitalism and was found to be most appropriate ideological counter to the feudal notion of divine right and unequal ascribed status. The modern democratic ideology has acted as the sustentaculum of this cultural ideal. None the less as the reproduction of capitalism demanded a different focus, the original formulation is eventually divested from the essence. The conception of natural inequality is recreated and the individual achievement in 'free' competition—instead of equal sharing of social products—is hailed as the panacean. Functionalism is the zenith of this discourse. Inequality is accordingly indispensable for the maintenance of social structure. A stupendous resuscitation of Aristotle !

Functionalism holds that structure of inequality (stratification) is ubiquitous, a generalized aspect of the structure of all social systems. Individuals differ in ability and it is through differential distribution of rewards, the society endeavours to ensure that the more qualified occupy the more important positions. Hence, social stratification is imperative and valuable to any social system (Parsons, 1954 : 92-108 ; Davis and Moore, 945). This anti-historical, anti-philosophical, mechanistic, positivistic and clearly apologetic approach has of course been variously criticised for over-emphasizing consensus (Dahrendorf 1959) and considering stratification as universal and permanent (Bottomore 1963). Nevertheless, functionalism maintains a prominent place in deliberations on equality. Though some of the original postulates of functionalism have since been amended and many permutations an dcombinations have been worked out, most sociologists and social anthropologists seem to stand united in opposition to Marx's proposition that the classes in the last analysis determine the inner logic of the working and dynamics of various types of society. Marxism holds that social relations are governed by laws which are specific to each mode of production, and that the mode of production is the primary determinant of inequality. This is unacceptable to academic anthropologists.

## ANTHROPOLOGISTS AT WORK

The issue of equality and inequality has constituted the hidden agenda of anthropology since its beginning (Diamond, 1974). This inequality, however, mostly referred to the ethnocentric 'we', the White (and Whiting) anthropologists versus 'they', the uncivilized, historic and internally homogeneous objects. In that sense, role of anthropology as an intellectual weapon of imperialism, neo-colonialism and counter revolution is not an aberration. None the less, the wealth of material collected by anthropologists from culturally different situations can be profitably used for a cross-cultural comparison and analysis of social inequality. Gerald D. Berremen's edited volume (1981) under critical review is one such praiseworthy exercise.

During the summer of 1978, twenty social anthropologists assembled at the famous castle in Austria to discuss social inequality. The outcome is this charming volume, *Social Inequality : Comparative and Developmental Approaches*, edited by G.D. Berreman (1981), the symposium organizer. The papers represent recognized and authoritative developments in the current repertoire of social inequality in social anthropology. It includes 'distinctively' anthropological approaches namely, comparative across the full range and varieties of human societies around the world, over the entire period of human existence, and analyse the phenomenon holistically as an integral and inseparable component of the total complex whole (xiii-XIV).[2] The editor provides a

2. All references to the volume under review is simply communicated by the page number as other details are obvious in the text.

conceptual framework for the study of inequality. Besides, there are two more theoretical papers. Of the twelve empirically based papers three deal with the problem in unstratified societies and two in socialist societies. They together straddle several theoretical divides and retain curiosity and adventurousness. Ideological implications of some of the papers and their theoretical postulates are explicit, while others dexterously shy away from a discussion of political significance. We shall, however, restrict ourselves to an assessment of broad themes which underpin the detailed discussions.

Berreman's broad framework, 'Social Inequality : A Cross Cultural Analysis', would be our crucial focus for the discourse, The working premises of Berreman's framework are that the inequality is a major social *problem* in the world, and it 'is at the root of the most immediate, fundamental and fateful threats facing humankind' (p. 35). For the continuation of society, drastic reduction of inequality between peoples and nations is necessary. And the other premise is that no theory of inequality is adequate enough unless it can comprehend all instances and dimensions. Both are laudable. And how far this framework succeeds or otherwise in the desired directions and in unison will get explicated in the following pages.

## UNIVERSALITY OF INEQUALITY : THE PRE-CLASS SOCIETIES

Social inequality, Berremen observes, is the social evaluation of whatever differences are regarded as relevant in a given society or situation, and that dominance goes with it. The absence of inequality and of dominance is, however, only a theoretical possibility, which is apparently not encountered empirically in human society (p. 8). In all known societies status is, unequally, distributed. Of course in some small non-food producing societies, the inequality is limited to dyadic and non-categorical prestige bases. The division of labour is almost exclusively on the basis of age, sex and personal characteristics. This type of organization is called unranked.[3] In contrast, when inequality is institutionalized into hierarchy of statuses and the system of unequal distribution of rewards depends on the position in the kinship system or based on specific activity (e.g. religious, military) the organization is called kin or role ranked organization. Food producing stateless societies and chiefdoms are characterized by such an organization. In sum, all non-class societies are ranked by unequal statuses.

Antithetical to this pansocial characterization of inequality is M. D. Caulfields' paper, 'Equality, Sex and Mode of Production'. Arguing against various anthropological theories of universal sex-oppression and structural and symbolic devaluation of women, she remarks that the essential and representative fact of most of these theories is the absence of a historical treatment of inequalities. The evidence buttressed in support of these theories are normally collected from the colonized peoples, as if they were virtually unchanged representatives of the past. This conception of the 'ethnographic present' is, in effect, a denial of historicity to the Third World, and deliberate concealment of the role of imperialism in the devaluation of status of women. It is difficult to conceive of untouched societies; everyone of them carry the imprint of distortions forced on them. And sex-oppression has been one of the major imports from western capitalism. She holds that the sexual division of labour has a totally different and non-oppressive significance in societies which are organized around the production of use values; Male domination appeared with the erosion, distortion, and near-annihilation of use value by class societies. It is only when equality is conceived in terms of exchange relations that the sexual division of labour appears to carry the necessary implication of hierarchy (see also O'Laughlin, 1977 : 21). She is, however, aware of the fact that exchange crucial element in all societies, but where the societies are organized around use values, the exchange

3. While Berreman approvingly follows Fried (1960), he prefers to call such society 'unranked organization' instead of Fried's term egalitarian society, on the ground that there are status differences. He contends that Weber's term status is more at issue than class (pp. 8-9). Fried, on the other hand argues that 'at the heart of an egalitarian society is a fundamental egalitarian economy' (1967:35).

is made 'not on the basis of measurement or the attempt to achieve an exact equivalence' but on the principle of what Sahlins called 'generalized reciprocity' (1972 : 193-194). The political significance of this myth of universal sex oppression is that it isolates women's devaluation from the process of change in modes of production, and restrict the women's movements to a struggle for 'equality of women under capitalist relations' (p 217).

Likewise, Richard B. Lee in her paper, 'Politics, Sexual and Non-sexual Egalitarian Society : The Kung San', shows a relatively equal role of the sexes in a foraging society, and find no support for a view of women in the 'state of nature' as oppressed or dominated by men or as subject to sexual exploitation at the hands of the males (p. 89). Women's participation in decision making processes is though uneven, the leaders themselves adhere to the image of the 'egalitarian redistributors' (cf. Harris, 1975 : 289), and

> ...their accumulation of material goods is never more and is often less than the average accumulation of the other households in their camp (p. 97).

This may be strange, but Lee hastens to add that central to foraging model of production is a lack of wealth accumulation and the social differentiation that accompanies it. Endorsing Marx and Engles' model of primitive communism, she says :

> A truly communal life is often dismissed as a utopian ideal to be endorsed in theory but unattainable in practice. But the evidence for foraging peoples tells us otherwise. A sharing way of life is not only possible but has actually existed in many parts of the world and over periods of time (p. 99).

Curiously, Berreman, notwithstanding his assumption of universality of inequality and domination, largely agrees with Caulfield and Lee that such societies do not entail sexual exploitation.

There are, however, a couple of papers in the volume which consider non-exploitative social relations in small-scale societies of hunters and gatherers as the romantic Rousseauian image of the primitive. P. L Newman's paper, 'Sexual Politics and Witchcraft in Two New Guinea Societies' analyses social inequality along sexual lines. Eric R. Wolf's 'The Mills of Inequality : A Marxist Approach', deserves serious attention. He considers social inequality not as phenomenon *sui generis* but as an accompaniment of the workings out of determinental modes of production. The relevant mode here is his 'kin-ordered' mode. In this mode, social labour is 'locked up' in particular relations between people; elders and juniors, seniors and cadets, members of high ranking and low ranking, men and women, original settlers and new comers and so on. He cites two examples of rebellions of juniors against elders in the transition from settled village life to hunting (Holder, 1970) and to the formation of slave-raiding non-kin *quilombos* (Miller, 1975). Wolf, thus, argues that 'they are replete with real inequalities and plagued by resulting tensions' (p. 55). Further he opines :

> Unlike societies built upon the tributary or capitalist mode, they lack the ability to aggregate and marshall social labour apart from particular relationships, and therefore they also lack the means of holding society together, internally and externally, by internal and external violence that ensures the continuity of class domination and contradictions (p. 55).

If nothing else, these papers in the volume represent the fruits of the intense theoretical debates in anthropology, specially of the last decade. While the functionalist position has remained more or less unchanged, there has been something like a 'Paradigm shift' in the Marxist analysis of the 'Primitive' societies. Though this fundamental rethinking in Marxism cannot claim to provide the definitive solutions to the problematic, but it certainly throws light on the issue and suggests fresh perspectives.

## THE MYTH OF CLASSLESS 'PRIMITIVE'

It is not only Wolf but several Marxist anthropologists have noticed status inequalities even in the simplest small scale societies (Meillassoux, 1973; Rose, 1968; Sahlins, 1963; Goldelier, 1977: 70-120; Rey, 1979; Terray, 1972). It is argued that in the so-called primitive societies though woman has access to social control due to her reproductive and economic functions, it was always man who exercised this control. In matrilineal systems, authority reverts to the woman's brother and the maternal uncle, while in patrilineal societies it reverts to father and husband. Thus, the relationship between sexes is fundamentally asymmetric and non-reciprocal. Reciprocity thus exists only between men. Similarly the distinction between elders and juniors, where the elders preside over the redistribution processes, control marriage relations, demographic reproduction and prestige giving goods, which re-inforce the dependence of the juniors, points out incipient classes and the antagonism among them.

But by using the term 'class' for such divisions in society, where the juniors are all destined to become elders in the normal operation of the social structure, the concept loses its analytical power to distinguish between societies. There is every reason to doubt the equation : inequality=exploitation, and more so, in-equality=class antagonism. These structuralist Marxists have argued that there are no primitive; only distinct social formations with the combination of at least two modes of production, one of which is dominant and the other subordinate. This formulation gravitates to the cognition of structure and underplays the internal dynamics of society. In addition, at least for analytical purposes, if the natural process of the development of society is not separated from the impact of exogeneous forces, it is difficult to understand not only the pre-historic past but also the relative autonomy of the systems and their independent potentialities (Pathy, 1984:12). Besides all the evidence is gathered from the societies which carry the imprint of colonial and non-colonial domination.

Critically reviewing the classical and conventional Marxist literature on the topic, Maurice Bloch (1983) contends that because of the simplistic characterisation of primitive society as the idyllic communal classless community, the Marxists in a sense, 'stopped being Marxists when they turned to primitive society'. He remarks that Marx held 'slavery being inherent in the family' and the universality of class relations in the *Forman*, *German Ideology*, and

*Communist Manifesto*. It was only Engels (?), through his *Origin of Family, Private Property and State* who presented the untenable view of classes primitive community (Bloch, 1983 : 54-55). But it is also worth remembering that in 1877, Engels himself had warned against those who hoped to find in primitive communities, the exact image of social equality. He wrote :

> In the oldest primitive communities equality of rights existed at most for members of the community; women, slaves and strangers were excluded from this equality as a matter of course (p. 117).

Discussing at length the organizing principles of Germanic and Slavonic tribal societies, they noted that primitive societies were not all fashioned on the same cast. There were critical differences among them. In fact, Marx insisted that there were multiple forms of common ownership with differences in community's right of ownership, individual's right over use and even possession, and different forms of common labour (or absence of it). At least, two major types were identified—the 'spontaneous community' marked by shared production and immediate distribution of the product according to need, and the 'early settled primitive community' corresponding to the anthropological term, tribe. Marks and Engels argued that 'the communal character appears as the pre-condition of the joint appropriation and use of the soil' and as 'a negative unity in relation to the outside world' (1979 : 86). And they often reiterated that the reasons of the transformation of such societies are largely internal (1979 : 296).

Conceding the fact that the nature of inequality in 'Primitive' society is as yet an unsettled issue, one tends to acknowledge the analytical power of Marxism as against the esoteric, ambiguous and over-generalized functionalist perspective of universal inequality. Anyway, anthropology, which should have been more at ease with its formulations regarding the unstratified societies, for that is its specialized field, amazingly lacks any consensus whatsover. K. M. Zaretsky, the rapporteiur of the symposium, exclaims that there was sharp disagreement on the issue of presence or absence of inequality in non-stratified societies. 'On the whole' the participants 'found it easier to discuss inequality in stratified rather than in unstratified societies' (p. 353). To us, the diversities and contrasts in the anthropological treatment of 'Primitive' society appear as a necessary pre-condition to greater comprehension of the issue of inequality.

## TYPES AND DIMENSIONS OF STRATIFICATION

Once again let us begin with Berreman's conceptual framework. Stratification is his principal interest, and here he hopes to make some 'original' contribution (p. 12). In stratified societies, all members are ranked relative to one another in terms of the Weberian class, status and power. The categories of people form social layer (!), hence, the term strata. He divides stratification into two basic models namely, status strata and class strata. The former is based on culturally specific criteria of differential honour, prestige, and privilege shared by members of particular social categories (caste, race, ethnic group etc.). The class strata is based on economic relationships shared by those within a stratum. The critical difference between the two lies on the perceived source, or locus, of the criteria by which membership and its associated status are assigned' (p. 13). In case of status strata membership is based on characteristics regarded as *intrinsic* to the individual comprising the stratum. Social class membership and ranking, by contrast, is based on attributes regarded as *extrinsic* to the people who comprise the class. So classes are not 'groups' but 'categories', while status strata are by nature groups. Berreman remarks here:

> Marxists have long been frustrated by the implications of this fact : Workers of the world have generally failed to unite—or even to feel common cause—especially when ethnic, race, or caste differences divide them (p. 18).

Berreman's way of extricating the Marxists, I suppose, is a focus on 'Association', like Weber's party or Lowie's sodality. The significance of association, which is a 'group' based on extrinsic criteria of economic relations whose members are conscious, lies in the fact that it is least tied to the rank principle and would thus be the source for elimination or drastic reduction of social stratification.

Before we proceed further into his framework, let us briefly reflect on his Weberian analysis and conception of class. The Weberian multivariate analysis of inequality which Berreman prefers to tread is basically a static model, without any scope for a dynamic account of the genesis and development of societies. There being no dynamic contradictions in the model, it can only comprehend the stable features of continuity of a prevailing order (Meszaros, 1972 : 42). Since no social phenomenon can properly be studied unless it is placed in the context of history, the Weberian treatment of inequality in their static aspects depicts false relations. The conception of class depends on the notion of 'life chances' which, in turn, are determined by the individual's relationship to markets of various kinds. In other words, it emphasizes how classes are produced as a result of the manner in which rewards are acquired and distributed. Thus, classes in Weberian sense are 'neither communities nor organized groups but simply aggregates of people possessing similar economic interest' (Mayer, 1955 : 24). The distributions are relations of competition and emulation expressed in the form of a continuum, *without any sharp break or conflict*. Social inequality is certainly multidimensional. Marx never implied otherwise—but there is a certain 'inner bond of relationships' among the dimensions in any given social context. These relationships influence one another not in equal but in unequal ways. Unessential and marginal phenomena recede into the background and are replaced by general, common, and increasingly abstract relationships, tendencies and regularities. Weberian methodology is incapable of unfolding these relationships and hence gives more or less equal emphasis to class, status and party. But it has reached a stage when it can no longer harp on the same string; it must proceed to establish the laws of social development.

The Marxist concept of class is distinctive in that it cannot be defined by reference to internal attributes, unlike the synthetic hierarchical gradation scheme so common in contemporary stratification literature. It is a relational concept, *i.e.* existing in relation to another class(es), either through struggle and opposition or through domination and bondage with it. It is formed historically in a continuous process of conflict and accommodation, and contextually refers to a relationship between sets of people in the productive process. The class structure is thus revealed by discerning the structure of exploitation, of appropriation and its negation as well as relative independence from both (Pathy, 1984 : 37-38). The operationalization of Marxist conception of class is, however, beset with a number of problems, especially in the pre-capitalist social formations, where the boundary tends to be rather ambiguous. Marx had noted that classes did not appear in a 'pure form' until the capitalist mode of production had established its hegemony. In pre-capitalist systems, there being non-economic bonds and relations of personal dependence between producers and the owners of the means of production, cannot be the sufficient principle of determining all inequalities (Terray, 1972 : 146-49). Besides, though class, class consciousness, and class action are facets of a single inextricably interwoven complex, for the purpose of analysis of social dynamics it is necessary to distinguish between the objective class from the conscious and active objective class (PrZeworski, 1974 : 348-367). Despite these difficulties, the Marxist concept of class does direct us correctly to understand the structure of inequality in class societies. Berreman's idealist concept of 'association' is no alternative to the difficulties mentioned in Marxist concept of class. We will have occasion to return to Berreman's concept once again.

Eric R. Wolf in his paper cited above gives the rationale for using the concept of mode of production in comparative anthropology. He discusses the concept of labour process, social formation, social interaction and cultural forms of mediating within and between various social formations. He observes that there are three broad ways in which human beings organize their social relations of production and their process of work. These correspond to three different modes of production—capitalist, tributary and kin-ordered. In concrete contexts these modes appear in combination. Thus, Wolf remarks: 'In the world studied by anthropologists. some of the most interesting problems concern the ways in which the expansion of one mode may reinforce or alter inequalities in the other' (p. 56). Though we have reservations on certain points, especially the characterization of 'Kin-ordered' mode, and dividing all modes into three without much elaboration, it does demonstrate the importance of studying class relations, for both understanding a system and deciphering the potentialities and directions of change.

Turning to Berreman's typology of stratification, it may be reiterated that for him *class* is defined by its being extrinsic to the people, as a category. The *association* is also extrinsic economic relations but is a group. *Caste* is a status strata, intrinsic to the individuals comprising the stratum, and is a group. *Race* is like caste but is category instead of group. *Ethnic group* is also a status strata but is defined by criteria of membership that are both extrinsic and intrinsic. Ethnicity is a product of learned cultural heritage rather than social and economic condition (p. 16). *Estate* is a class strata defined by both intrinsic and extrinsic criteria and is a category. In short this 'comparative analytical framework' considers three principle dimensions of statification, namely, the Weberian status and class division, the anthropological conception of emic and etic to differentiate social groups from social categories, and the source of the characteristics employed in designating the membership, *i.e.* intrinsic or extrinsic. Following Mertonian 'reference group theory', Berreman holds that 'associations', ethnic groups and castes are usually easily mobilized for perceived interests of their members than are classes, estates and races. Of course, the 'associations' being the unranked systems are most suited for bringing about planned change. It seems while working within an essentially functionalist—Weberian framework of stratification, he hopes to contribute/develop the Marxian perspective of social change. In the process, the motive force of history is reduced to associations and clubs. This is no solution to the Weberian bankruptcy. It has reached a stage when it can no longer harp on the same string; it must proceed to establish the laws of social development. Unfortunately, the author claims too much for his formalistic framework. The outcome is highly syncretistic and eclectic, which has considerably reduced its explanatory capacity. He evades the necessity of historical reflection. There is a strange silence of any serious examination of the Marxist contributions. If he would have incorporated the Marxist conception of social class, instead of the Weberian bourgeois conception of class, he could have explored the historic significance of the concept. That there have been major social upheavals, both historically and contextually, could have been acknowledged. And the role played by other differences to obstruct the process of social dynamics might have been outlined. But it is difficult to anticipate so much from some one who is reluctant to go beyond the stratification perspective. The framework being essentially enshrined in the existential—hermeneutics, is pitched without consideration of magnitudes, timing, and political and social forces involved.

Let us ponder a while over his typology. The remark that ethnicity is not a result of socio-economic condition but a product of cultural heritage, reflects his deliberate neglect of ethnic history of the world. Beneath ethnicity lies the general context of inequality in which ethnic relations operate. The unresolved socio-economic problems are the root causes of inter-ethnic friction (Banks and Gay, 1978) In order to remedy the situation, it is necessary to modify the structure of a society as well as the ideological system of an international and national social system, of which gross inequality is the characteristic (Bonacich, 1979 ; Portes, 1978 ; Saul, 1979). To deny the material basis of ethnicity is to conceal the reality.

Stratification theorists have generally considered estates as a separate category. It is distinguished through differential immunities defined in law, *i.e.* legal inequalities. But in the Marxist framework there is no need to discuss estate as a separate type, for it is basically a feature of feudal system (Bloch, 1931). With regard to caste, Berreman claims to have incorporated 'evolutionary processes and sequences within' the framework (p. 24). He remarks that caste is not specific to India.

> Indian caste system comprises a unique congruity among kin, status, rank, occupation, class, culture and power, creating a

> powerful, involute, and total system of stratification . . . . But it is *not* well suited to complex, rapidly changing urban-industrial organization . . . . True class stratification is thus becoming more prominent (p. 26).

Further, Berreman holds that the *jajmani* relations between the castes suggest its equivalency to the European estate relations (p. 28). There are at least two papers which accept Berreman's near-universality of caste system. Schuyler Jones in his, 'Institutionalised Inequalities in Nuristan' finds that in the north-east Afghanistan the nature and ordering of social classes closely resemble caste system of India. The other paper, 'Education, Clientage and Social Mobility : Caste and Social Change in the United States and Nigeria', is by John U. Ogbu. The author argues that the racial stratification in the United States satisfies Berreman's definition of caste system as a hierarchy of endogamous group whose membership is determined permanently at birth. So, also the case of Igbos of Nigeria. In both cases, pace of status mobility (occupational) through education and 'collective Clientage' has increased for the subordinate 'castes'. And he anticipates that very soon.

> Blacks and Whites will eventually be participating in one status mobility system dominated by a single institutionalized strategy—educational credentials—a situation that will eliminate the social mobility gap between the two racial groups (p. 278).

And so also the caste groups among the Igbos. A fond functionalist hope indeed ; as if the only source of inequality is education and the consequent occupational status.

These studies do not acknowledge the historical specificity of caste system. It is true that systems analogous to caste marked by certain features are found elsewhere but that does not raise caste as a universal and generalized form in humankind. Indian scholars are aware of the debate, mainly originating with Western scholarship's divided consideration of caste as a cultural phenomenon versus a structural form. Among others, Johnson, Cox, Leach, Myrdal, Ryan, Sorokin and Dumont hold that caste is peculiar to India, mainly for its specific cultural complexity. Whereas Berreman,

Barth, Bailey, Carstairs. Davis, Harper, Nadel, Tumin, Donoghue, Chapple and Coon, Gallaghar and even Meillassoux consider that the caste system is spread over large areas. The former is an idealist, Brahminical view which in effect gives tacit approval to the racial conquest theory, and reinforces the mystical and romanticized notion about the uniqueness of the Indian society. The later advances untenable, speculative hypotheses on the similarities between caste and race, and caste and estate. In both cases, the materialist base (Meillassoux is an exception) is absent and a scenario of traditionally fixed statuses and occupations, of hierarchy and social immobility is evoked. But the unity of both aspects in the systems of production is hardly attemped Morton Klass, strongly refuting much of the existing theories of caste, outlines a Marxist perspective that caste is the concrete system of interrelated and co-existing marriage circles. The whole society, being composed of such groups, exclusion from a group means exclusion from the total society. Hence, castes are endogamous groups, but are interconnected primarily through exchange of economic goods or services (1980 : Chaps V and VII; also the review Sharma 1983). The view that caste is changing to class is again more a reflection of ethnocentric propaganda than truth. Class has always existed alongwith caste as an inseparate, largely congruent phenomenon of social inequality in India (Thapar, 1974 : 95-123). And that caste has shown remarkable changes within, over the years.

Berreman discusses age, sex, stigmatization and servitude as residual categories as those cannot fit into his framework (p 24). In stratified societies, age and sex differences are closely allied with other forms of stratification. Stigmatization and consequent assignment of low status to various categories of peoples in complex societies like physical handicaps, social stereotypes, illegal professionals etc. is too widespread and difficult to compare and generalize. Servitude includes indentured labour, bonded labour, serfdom and slavery. This status is not linked to particular task or occupation, not subject to degree of negotiability and independence of action. When it is birth ascribed it becomes a form of caste or race, when it is ethnically ascribed it becomes a form of ethnic group, and when it is the result of economic or political events (like debt or capture), it can be extreme form of class (pp. 23-24). As if, servitude can ever be independent of economic and political domination of class. This category, seen from the Marxist point of view includes not only the subject classes of an ancient period but also feudal and capitalist context and its analytical capacity is weak and does not tell us anything about the social system within which the servitude as a relation appears. Berreman is tuned to the functionalists who normally consider slavery and estate as two of the four principal types of stratification.

## NATURAL INEQUALITY

There are some papers in the volume which deal with certain d mensions of stratification, but Berreman's framework does not reflect them, at least not directly. One such is Andre Peteille's paper titled, 'The idea of Natural Inequality'. Though Berreman approvingly refers to this paper. he does not elaborate. Beteille rightly points out that in advanced industrial societies (or capitalist countries) there is a widespread belief in natural ordering of individuals which can be revealed only through fair and free competition. In fact, Caulfield in her paper cited above puts the point more sharply. The ideal of equality in the capitalist system with rewards and competition is predicted on an extreme inequality. It 'is intimately tied with the ideology of bourgeois rationality and the denial of affect or collectivity in one's relations to the productive or distributive (market) process' (p. 203). Beteille on the other hand implicitly rationalizes such inequality. He contends that the insights of Rousseau and Locke on the distinction between state of nature and state of society. or between nature and culture, 'calls for a fresh examination of the presumed basis of inequality in human societies' (p. 64). Why ? Because 'the division of labour as it exists in any human society entails certain inequalities of status and power among the differentiated parts or positions' (p. 66). And here Beteille wants to take Marx and Engels to task. He says that although, they held division of labour, class, and inequality as inseparably linked, but as they did not concede that the division of labour was a necessary (natural) condition of social existence, the solution to the problem of class and inequality is difficult to comprehend. He says that since every culture evaluates and discriminates it is hard to conceive of a society without division of labour. It may be recalled that Marx (1867) had remarked that the division of labour by sex and age in pre-class society was a 'technical' division, in which social agents are distributed into socially equivalent places in production. It is only 'social' division of labour which characterises relations of exploitation in class societies (1970 : 351). The divisions of labour are determined by the development of productive forces. In class societies, the division of labour is interwoven with class antagonisms.

Anyway, Beteille's message is clear when he commends Durkheim that 'just society is simply that where social inequalities exactly express natural inequalities' (p. 71). This is in the line arguments of T. H. Huxley and Francis Galton who sought to prove that natural inequality is the bedrock on which all inequalities rest. Hence he says : 'It is difficult to see how one can deny some role to genetic factors in the perpetuation of individual variations' (p. 76). Though there are not much formal theoretical and logical articulation of this point of view, 'two hundred fifty million test scores serve to make a point more effectively than any formal theory of natural inequality could hope to do' (p. 78). The neologisms and allusive argument in the paper conceal an approximation to the theoretical traditions of Huxley and Galton. Implicit is a rationalization of the present unequal and unjust order. By extension, individual himself is held responsible for his position. Anyway, inequality can hardly be taken as a part of the natural order of things.

Almost all the other papers go against the natural explanation of inequality. A special mention may be made of two papers. Bernard Magubane in his paper, 'Social Inequality : the South African Case', conceptualizes racial inequality as an aspect of imperialism and colonialism. He asserts that the development of racism was not based on natural law but on given historical circumstances. Racial oppression and class exploitation are inextricably intertwined in the modern world. Racism as a formal, ideological system is cultivated by the politically conscious classes to subvert class unity between Black and White labour (p. 275).

Likewise, Sydel Silverman's paper, 'Rituals of Inequality: Stratification and Symbol in Central Italy' question the congruence between symbols and social categories. Among others, Bloch has questioned the same (1974, 71-77); but Silverman's central concern is to show the relationship of various ritual symbolic categories to class—which he rightly thinks as the framework within which other social distinctions exist—and explore the implications of the symbolic phrasing of inequality for the class structure. He notes that the symbolic contrast between sexes, acts to obscure and defuse socio-economic cleavages (p. 170). Age inequality, however, being cyclical, has only a limited utility for defueling class antagonisms. Considering other aspects he observes that "the social distinctions 'expressed' in ritual obliterate fundamental socio-economic realities" (p. 180). And further, cultural use of social distinctions in ritual and symbol cannot be understood only in 'cultural' terms, 'but must be seen as determinate results of historically rooted political and economic processes' (p. 180).

In contrast to Silverman's paper, in a simplistic way, Peter Worsley, in his paper 'Social class and Development' argues that until Marxism develops an adequate theory of culture, irrespective of its power in the field of the analysis of economic relations, it 'will remain less capable than bourgeois social science of handling the interplay between economic and non-economic relations' (p. 249). Obviously, his criticism of functionalism is no more than an eyewash. Except for repeating unfounded assertions, Worsley's paper not only lacks any alternative design but also a critical insight. His accusation against Marxism for its vision of an inevitable and 'fairly speedy transition' to a class conscious 'for itself' via class struggle has been played nth times in anti-Marxist literature.

Two more papers need a brief mention. Martin Oran's 'Hierarchy and Happiness in a Western Samoan Community' considers that happiness—satisfaction and good life evaluations in various domains like wealth, income and mobility by the members is more revealing and best way to depend on for the study of inequality. Suffice here to note that there is always systematic discrepancy between the structure of class and the subjective representation of hierarchy by the people themselves (Bloch, 1977). Behaviouralism and opinion polls can indicate the structure, and much less the potentiality for dynamics of a system. The only exception periods could be those when the people themselves in organized scientific way fight against inequality.

J. H. Bodley in his paper, 'Inequality : An Energetics Approach' presents energy inequality as a tool for comparative study of inequality. He notes that the overall per capita energy level of a culture does seem to be a significant variable influencing the nature of inequality (p. 185). He holds that low energy cultures are those with less than 26000 kilo calories of per capita energy consumption, mostly in the form of renewable and non-commercial. It is, however, by now well-established that averaging of income, which paradoxically it seeks to explore. Bodley's case study on village India is pertinent : 'The overall trend in India since 1953 has been toward an increasing energy inequality' (p. 196). He pleads that minimum energy allowance should be recognized as a basic human right (p. 196). A noble idea ! But declaration of this in principle by United Nations hardly assure its implementation. How many basic human rights and to what increasing extent have been violated can even be seen from the World Bank documents on starvation, malnutrition, poverty, illiteracy, unemployment and so on. Those rights are essentially political issues, which can be resolved primarily through political struggles by the deprived and dominated people themselves. Declaration of minimum energy allowance may yield little in the given world system.

## INEQUALITIES IN SOCIALIST SOCIETIES

Two papers in the volume consider the issue of stratification in socialist societies. Martin King Whyte writes on 'Destratification and Restratification in China', and with special reference to Poland,

WlodZimierz Wesdowski and Tadeusz Krauze write, 'Socialist Society and the Meritocratic principle of Remuneration'. By now there is massive literature on discovering the inequalities in Soviet society.[4] Whyte accordingly argues that there is little evidence and support to the proposition that socialism leads to increased social equality. Instead, socialist regimes 'have shown a tendency to introduce new and complex forms of inequality and concentration of power' (p. 309). And this proves the functionalist view of essentiality of structured inequality. He labours to point out that during Cultural Revolution in China (1966-69), though there was an attempt to eliminate ranks in institutions, reduce privileges, prestige and favourable mobility opportunities of advantaged groups in society, the new leadership after Mao's death has dismantled the egalitarian reforms of the previous decade. It has now emphasised educational quality and standards and the privileges between urban-rural, cadre-worker and mental-manual labour have widened. Like functionalists Chinese leadership is said to be propagating that material, power and status differentials are functional and necessary (p. 326). Hence Whyte remarks :

> . . . . the Chinese case can no longer be pointed to as evidence that the functionalist arguments are wrong, and that socialism can provide a formula for realizing economic development without compromising the commitment to social equality (p. 332).

The logic seems to be crude. Where did Marx or Engels say that there would be complete equality in socialist society? Socialist society contains several non-antagonistic classes—the working class, the collective farm peasantry, and the intelligentsia. There are essential distinctions between town and country, and between mental and physical labour. Material wealth is distributed according to the principle, 'From each according to his work'. The constraints imposed

4. The well known works are those of Milovan Djilas, S. Ossowski, Raymond Aron, T. B. Bottomore, Alex Inkels, P. Bellis, David Lane, J. Burnham, Peter Wiles, Barrington Moore, *et al.* For reasons of space, we prefer to avoid the references.

on the ideal of equity in the socialist society is historical, depending on the level of development of productive forces. Marx thus said :

> The right of the producers is proportional to the labour they supply : the equality consists in the fact that measurement is made with an equal standard, labour . . . . But one man is superior to another physically or mentally and so supplies more labour in the same time, or can labour for longer time; and labour, to serve as a measure, must be defined by its duration or intensity otherwise it ceases to be a standard of measurement. This equal right is an unequal right for unequal labour (1938 : 9).

It is only in the communist system that the divisions between peasantry and working class, rural and urban population, manual and non-manual labour, and differences associated with various trades, skills, and incomes can be eliminated. For then, distribution of social wealth would be governed by the principle, 'To each according to his needs', Nonetheless, there would be little dispute to acknowledge the facts that under socialism the private ownership of the means of production has been abolished, the income pyramid flattened, free and equal access to education broadened, the differences between different types of labour decreased, and the fundamental relations of power and property changed. All these together point to greater equality than the so-called neutral and value-free scholars across the disciplines would like to convey. This however does not mean that the existing socialist societies are perfect models of socialism. But that is altogether a different area to deliberate on.

The authors on Poland have convincingly argued that there is a close association and considerable conceptual proximity between meritocratic principle of remuneration, though both cannot be equated. In socialist society,

> . . .differentiation of pay based on education and skill is perceived as being legitimate, superior to, and more just than that based on private capital, the arbitrary personal assessment of managers, or pure political power. The prevalent

egalitarian ethos in Poland does not affect the meritocratic principle as such but it may decrease the range of pay (p. 348).

## PLANNED CHANGE

Returning to Berreman's conceptual framework, we may reiterate that for him 'associations' are most important to a planned change towards the elimination or drastic reduction of social stratification. Besides, there ought to be attempts to minimize the accumulation and privileged economic access as a means to status achievement, and to eliminate class and all stratification. He finds that the cultural revolution phase in Chinese socialism corresponds to most of his suggestions. Chinese made efforts to turn stratification to a kind of role ranking, minimized accumulation, emphasized sharing and redistribution, eliminated intrinsic criteria for social differentiation, minimized class differences and stratification, focussed on small groups and moved away from specialists to generalists. But neither Berreman refers to the process of how these changes have been made possible nor brings forth the principle and coherence of the Chinese efforts. Much less detailed is how his anarchist, a historic concept of 'association' with emphasis on individual consciousness and spontaneity is compatible to the revolutionary struggles of the Chinese people. Nonetheless, he agrees that in socialist societies, specially in China, social inequality is low. And thereby he acknowledges the inevitable, albeit hesitatingly.

Given the heterogeneity of theoretical orientations and methodological prescriptions, and entrenched ethical and political overtone of a certain idealist tradition, the prospect of comparative and developmental approaches to social inequality is not very promising. But the different perspectives and points of view presented in the volume denote the recent strength of anthropology is not taking things for granted. This is a very healthy sign. It needs hardly a mention here that the volume is inherently provocative and stimulating for the students and researchers of anthropology and related disciples.

## *REFERENCES*


Aristotle, 1959. *Politics and Athenian Constitution.* London : J. M. Dent.

Banks, J. A. and G. Gay. 1978. 'Ethnicity in Contemporary American Society: Towards a Development of a Typology', *Ethnicity*, V(3) : 238-251.

Berreman, Gerald D. (ed.), 1981. *Social Inequality : Comparative and Development Approaches.* New York : Academic Press.

Bloch, Marc, 1931 Feudalism : European', in R. A. Seligman (ed.) *Encyclopedia of the Social Sciences.* New York : Macmillan. VI : 203-210.

Bloch, Maurice, 1974. Symbols, Song, Dance and Features of Articulation : Is Religion an Extreme Form of Religious Authority ?' *European Journal of Sociology*. XV : 55-81.

——, 1977. 'The Disconnection between Power and Rank as a Process', *European Journal of Sociology*, XVIII : 107-148.

——, 1983. *Marxism and Anthropology : The History of a Relationship* Oxford : Clarendon Press.

Bonacich, Edna, 1980. 'Class Approaches to Ethnicity and Race,' *The Insurgent Sociologist*, X(2) : 9 24.

Bottomore, T. B., 1963. *Classes in Modern Society.* London : George Allen and Unwin.

Dehrendorf. Ralf. 1959. *Class and Class Conflict in Industrial Society*. Stanford : University Press.

Davis, K. and W. E Moore, 1945. 'Some Principles of Stratification,' *American Sociological Review*, X(2) : 242-49.

Diamond, Stanley. 1974. *In Search of the Primitive : A Critique of Civilization.* New Jersey : Transaction Books.

Engels, Frederick, 1939. *Anti-Duhring*. New York : International Publishers (First edition 1877).

Ferguson, N., 1968. *An Essay on the History of Civil Society.* London : Miller and Cadell (First edition 1967).

Fried, Morton, 1960. 'On the Evolution of Social Stratification and the State', in Stanley Diamond (ed.), *Culture and History: Essay in Honour of Paul Radin.* New York : Columbia University Press.

——, 1967. *The Evolution of Political Society*. New York : Random House.

Godelier, Maurice, 1977. *Perspectives in Marxist Anthropology*. Cambridge : Cambridge University Press.

Harris, Marvin, 1975 *Culture, People, Nature*. New York: Thomas Y. Crowell.

Holder Preston, 1970. *The Hoe and the Horse on the Plains*. Lincoln : University of Nebraska Press.

Klass, Morton, 1980. *Caste : The Emergence of the South Asia Social System*. Philadelphia . The Institute for the Study of Human Issues.

Marx, Karl, 1938. *Critique of the Gotha Programme*. New York International Publishers (First edn. 1875):

——, 1970. *Capital*. Vol. I. London : Lawrence and Wishart: (First edn. 1867).

——, and F. Engels, 1979. *Pre-capitalist Socio-Economic Formations*. Moscow : Progress Publishers.

Mayer, K. B , 1955. *Class and Society*. New York : Doubleday and Company.

Meillassoux, Claude, 1973. 'On the Mode of Production of the Hunting Band', in P. Alexandre (ed.), *French Perspectives in African Studies*. London : Oxford University Press.

Meszaros, Istvan, 1972. 'Ideology and Social Science', *The Socialist Register*. London : The Merlin Press.

Millar, John, 1971. 'The Origin of the Distinction of Ranks,' reprinted in W. C. Lehman (1960), *John Millar of Glasgow*. Cambridge : Cambridge University Press.

Miller, J. C. 1975. *Kings and Kinsmen : Early Moundu States in Angola*. London : Oxford University Press.

O'Laughlin, Bridget, 1977. 'Production and Reproduction ; Meillassoux's Femmes', *Critique Anthropology*, III(8).

Parsons, Talcott, 1954. 'A Revised Analytical Approach to Theory of Social Stratification,' in R. Bendix and S. M. Lipset (eds.), *Class Status and Power*. London : Routledge and Kegan Paul.

Pathy, Jaganath, 1948. *Tribal Peasantry : Dynamics of Development*. New Delhi : Inter-India Publications.

Portes, Alejandro, 1978. 'Migration and Underdevlopment,' *Politics and Society*, VIII (1).

Przeworski, Adam, 1974. 'Proletariat into Class', *Politics and Society*, VII (4) : 348-367.

Rey, P. P., 1979. 'Class Contradiction in Lineage Societies,' *Critique of Anthropology*, IV (13, 14) : 41-60.

Rose, F. G. G., 1968. 'Australian Marriage, Land Owning Groups, and Invitations', in R. Lee amd I. Devore (eds.), *Man the Hunter*. Chicago : Aldine.

Rousseau, J. J., 1912. *A Dissertation on the Origin and Foundation of Inequality of Mankind*. London : Everyman edition.

Sahlins, Marshally, 1963. 'Poor Man, Rich Man, Big Man, Chief : Political Types in Melanesia and Polynesia', *Comparative Studies in Society and History*, V (3) : 285-393.

——, 1972. *Stone Age Economics*. Chicago : Aldine.

Saul, J. S., 1979. 'The Dialectic of Class and Tribe', *Race and Class*, XX(4) : 347-372.

Sharma, S. P., 1983. 'A Materialist thesis on the Origin and Continuity of the Caste System in South Asia', *The Eastern Anthropologist*, 36(1) : 55-78.

Terray; Emmanuel, 1972. *Marxism and Primitive Societies : Two Studies*. New York : Review Press.

Thapar, Romila, 1974. 'Social Mobility in Ancient Indian Society', in R. S. Sharma (ed.), *Indian Society : Historical Probing*. New Delhi : Peoples Publishing House.

# 3

# SOCIAL ANTHROPOLOGY IN INDIA : A COMMENT

> Of what use is an intellectual of published technique, if he evades his responsibility towards the problems of his time and the duties of his metier and his very quality as a man ?
>
> *A. Aguilar* (*1968 : 34*)

IN THE LAST four decades, scores of appraisals have been made on the health of Indian anthropology. Most of these conveyed an exaggerated potentiality of the subject and judged the relevance in terms of its contributions to the successful implementation of the state policies. As an important substantiation of the point, we are informed of the phenomenal growth of the discipline. There are about two dozen university departments of anthropology, and a dozen tribal research institutes. Professional associations, journals, publications, doctoral dissertations, and research reports pertaining to anthropology have certainly expanded many fold. Massive and generous support from government and foreign agencies for anthropological research is said to be another proof of the rising status of the subject. For the time being, we wish to share the optimism but, for the fact that the pointed unprecedented growth of anthropology in India is more or less equally experienced by nearly all other disciplines.

A minority of the reviews, in contrast, considered the subject as practiced, moribund. The critical remarks emerged out of the

Indian anthropological bias for a historical, non-economic and micro-research. Judged from the point of conceptual creativity, theoretical advancement, methodological refinements, and more particularly analytical handling out of the gut issues of the contemporary Indian social reality, social anthropology in India reveals a grotesque existence. Its vision is constricted, scope trivial, and analyses partial and superficial. Western reference models continue to flourish without any critical scrutiny. At least privately many would tend to agree with this set of views, but the explanation to the prevalent is missing and therefore, fail to provide an outline of the feature prospects of the subject.

Anthropology, like other social sciences, is historically and socially conditioned. To ignore this simple truth makes an appraisal incapable of comprehending the subject in its totality, and thereby, either evades the fundamental issues at stake or advances esoteric explanations. Rarely does an anthropologist ask why his discipline is preoccupied with trivial and irrelevant issues; how the subject is exposed to neo-colonialist domination; and why it is often said to be a *status quo* oriented discipline. Objective answers to these and other questions would unfold the ideology of the discipline and emerging self-criticism would enrich the subject and make it more relevant. It may be added, as a general rule, social scientists, cannot completely dissociate themselves from political beliefs and ideology. They are, thus, both social analysts and political propagandists. The proportion and the emphasis of the latter may vary from time to time, place to place, person to person, and discipline to discipline, but percolation of values and ideology to the scholarly works is, in a sense, inescapable. Those who claim to be able to divorce from political beliefs are nurturing at best a self-deception, at worst a conscious obfuscation. The problem, however, becomes serious when pet ideology and value promises take command over the ongoing scientific inquiry. In order to provoke discussion, we are making an attempt here to expose the ideological roots of social anthropology in India, as reflected in the major spheres of anthropologist's research in India.

It is a well-known fact that anthropology as a distinct discipline originated and flourished along with the process of expansion and consolidation of colonial imperium. The *raison d'etre* for anthropology was to facilitate colonial administration by discovering ways of governing and controlling the colonised people. Anthropology provided a multidimensional contribution to colonialism. Alien administration required knowledge of the culture, social organization, customary law, and power structure of the subjugated people. Anthropology provided the expertise. The second dimension was not the simple administration for its own sake but for expropriation of the native material and human resources, and expansion of unequal exchanges. Hitherto the immobile working force had to be conditioned so that they could be easily recruited for the profitable mines, plantations, and armed forces. Ethnographic accounts are once again essential. Besides, to counteract any upsurge or revolt against external domination, it was necessary to provide a set of fragmentary images of the people, and thereby deny existence of a national identity. And in order to establish hegemony, it was necessary to articulate their interests through the local reactionary classes and strata, as well as to propagate technological and cultural superiority. The type of esoteric interests of anthropologists and their exaggeration of the segmentary and pluralistic foci of the colonised societies through the details of the diversity of the customs in different segments of the population conveyed disunity among the people and was one of the major stumbling blocks of national independence struggles. As elsewhere, in India, these studies were oriented towards denying the identity of India as a nation. The tribes were considered distinct, correlated units from the cases, one linguistic group from other linguistic groups, village from towns etc. This contributed to the 'divide and rule' policy of the colonial regimes. Articulation of the colonial interests by co-opting the local pre-capitalist force helped the regime from being directly the target of confrontation. Sometimes, this 'indirect rule' was however, partially altered to meet the requirements of colonial capital. Whenever there was movement, particularly with nation movement, the ideology of superiority too, was reverted to romantic idealisation of indigenous cultures and institutions and portrayed a happy society with commitments to their preservation In the following discussion our interest is confined to the evaluation of the changes that have appeared in specific fields of social of anthropological interests during the post-colonial period.

**Tribal Studies**

Many thought that anthropological association with colonialism, would not allow the discipline to grow in the post-colonial milieu. But soon the despair appeared unfounded. The very nationalist leadership, who were critical of the nature of tribal studies, in f ct, gave impetus to an ever-rising interest in tribal research.

In ancient Indian literature, there was no equivalent for the English term tribe. The people were either unconscious of their ethno-national identities, or called themselves as "People" vs. outsiders, in their own distinctive speech. During the nineteenth century, colonialism faced formidable challenges from those "peoples" who were later named as tribes. In the course of time, a few food gathering communities and shifting cultivators were also added to the list of tribes and soon tribe as a social category, distinct from the Hindus and the Muslims got crystallized through an oversimplified notion that the former were animists while the latter were not. All these communities were given different fictitious names. In 1981, they numbered about 22 million. To the nationalists. these moves of the British appeared as one of the sinister designs to obstruct national consolidation and the movement for independence.

With independence the hiatus between tribes and castes is sanctified by the Constitution. And over the years, due to political compulsions, internal ethnic divisions and phonetic variations, the number of tribes have increased from 212 in 1950 to more than 427 now and they constitute about 7.5 per cent of the Indian population (42 million). In short, the tribe in India is basically a politico-administrative category, and has little objective socio-cultural or economic connotation. But the anthropologists, who until recently were *de facto* tribal researchers, have uncritically accepted the administrative category. For all the tribal researchers of today, a tribe is a tribe which is included in the official list of scheduled tribes. A few years back, there were some attempts to define the tribe, but the definitions were not only dissimilar but even contradictory to one another. This could not have been otherwise for the definitions were made on the basis of one or two communities already notified as tribes. If the common indicators are only taken into consideration, then excluding a dozen or so small communities, the rest of those listed under the scheduled tribes category cannot be called tribes (Pathy, *et al.*, 1976). Hence, the least that is expected is the identification of the most important and necessary denominator, which not only characterises the community but also determines its transformation, i.e. if that factor changes, the system itself tends to change. This is no easy job; but it has been made more difficult by uncritical acceptance or a *Priori* administrative category as the social space. Besides, as in the colonial period, the definitions tended to distinguish the tribe from the caste. Its political connotations apart, the inability to transcend and embrace what is universal in human experience is too glaring to mention.

In addition to the problem of definition and identification of tribe, there are several inherent axiomatic propositions in Indian tribal studies, which hinder scientific understanding of primitive societies. The notion's communes with regards to the tribes have been that, they are (a) isolated and closed entities due to their unique historical and cultural setting; (b) a historic and static societies, surviving as a "cultural lag"; (c) homogeneous and ins-tructured units of production and consumption; (d) being backward, are exploited by the non-tribals; and (e) because of, every tribe tends to benefit more or less equally from a given policy and expenditure of the state extended towards the tribals. The concrete reality of the officially declared and academically groomed tribes in India, however, cannot share such romantic notions (Pathy, 1982). The scope does not permit us to deal with this to any great length. Suffice here to say, that isolation is so relative and unique setting so non-substantive, that an assumption based on these is not only simply nadequate but also misleading and fallacious to a very considerable extent. Notwithstanding the information to the contrary, Indian anthropology is still unprepared to change its colonially inherited delusive assumption of homogeneous tribes. The so-called tribes in India have largely been a part of the Indian society for a long time, and therefore can hardly be cognizable in a separate context.

What about tribal social dynamics ? The institution is largely seen as a shift from tribe to caste. Supposing we agree with this, how do we then explain the every growing tribal ethnic movements, manifest contradictions between tribes and non-tribes, and the premise of non-tribal exploitation itself ? To a very considerable extent the approach has succumbed to the specificity of the Indian caste system, which incidentally is another overriding area of anthropological interest. As a consequence, the intellectual insight into the process of transformation of tribal societies is blurred. The secular dimension of change in the tribal societies is located purely in the exogenous factors, more specifically policies of tribal welfare and theories of diffusion and modernization.

## CASTE STUDIES

During the colonial period, various speculative and untenable theories were put forward to account for these origins of caste and their historical development. Every anthropologist was trained to study social organization and religious beliefs and practices They sought to make contributions to cultural history on the basis of collection and comparison of customs and values of different castes. However, the bulk of caste studies included simple descriptive and ethnographic material. The occasional interest to interpret the data was always done with a functionalist framework, uncritically borrowed from Britain.

After independence, caste studies are marked by an emphasis on intensive fieldwork. They covered functional interdependence of castes, purity and pollution, nature and types of caste mobility, forms of dependence and dominance between castes, and intercaste frictions. Whatever concepts Indian anthropology has contributed are mainly related to the culture of castes "Sanskritization," hierarchical levels of interacting cultural traditions : "universalization and parochialization" are primarily focused on understanding of culture and cultural changes. Certain models like "little and great traditions" and "bridge action" are minor acceptions, which tried to establish connections between various cultural sub-systems as well as so far compartmentalized units like tribe and caste. For the structure of castes, there are only descriptive categories like "dominant caste," and "caste, class and power."

By and large, studies on caste systems and the concepts developed for their analysis take for granted the rationality of the economic system, and are concerned more for values and norms than anything else. Caste status is considered most important while patterns of land distribution and land relations are of secondary or tertiary importance. The implicit assumption is that in India, the individual has little autonomy of his own, except as a member of an ascriptive group. This is a legacy of colonial anthropology, and unfortunately even now there is no serious move to challenge the unscientific assumptions. Essentially these studies divert attention from the fundamental contradictions and problems in the system and seek to bring to a turbulent situation.

## VILLAGE STUDIES

The British administration had encouraged investigation of the village communities and the system of land tenure to facilitate revenue collection. The nationalist struggle also demanded investigation into the problems of land alienation and depeasentisation. But it was only since the mid 1950s anthropological researches on Indian villages began. Several volumes of village studies were produced, hailing the functional method of analysis. The essential and representative fact of all these studies is that they are anti-historical, anti-philosophical, mechanistic and positivistic. Their approach to the social reality is atomistic and nominalistic. The guiding assumptions are that society is a relatively persisting configuration of elements, and that the consensus is the essential element of the social system. Change is treated as a gradual and cumulative process of adjustment to new situations and the source is considered largely external. The descriptive, microscopic single village studies—with some macroscopic treatise tending to revert to indology—gave rise to *ad hoc* and idiosyncratic generalisations; ironically, with a consistent neglect of the persistent and general phenomena. Class is almost always considered unimportant for the analysis and understanding of Indian society.

## DEVELOPMENTAL STUDIES

Anthropological concern for development has so far been confined to a few spheres like tribal welfare, community development, and modernization. The leaders of the Indian National Congress, who were very critical of the colonial special provision for tribes, expanded the preferential treatment to the tribals. As many as twenty articles and two special schedules concerning tribal welfare are enshrined in the Constitution.

Be that as it may, the dominant proposition in most of the tribal welfare studies has been the treatment of the conferment of privileges on the tribals, as a humanitarian concern of the state, and a repayment of historical debt. It is certainly an elementary and surface explanation. In addition, a mere glance at the actual expenditure for the tribals raises doubt at the over-popularised belief that a considerable finance of the state is diverted for the tribal welfare. Though they constitute more than seven per cent, the plan outlay for tribal welfare has always remained less than one per cent of the budget. There, too, only one-fourth is used for economic development, and even Government reports acknowledge the tribal rich have benefited the most from these privileges.

It may be recalled that most of the numerically well as economically important tribal groups, were among the earliest communities in India, who fought against expansion of colonialism and made the greatest sacrifices. Independent India could have hardly afforded to ignore their military. Deliberate attempts were made to avoid such "unpleasant" occurrences in future. But due to the political economy of stagnation and primitive accumulation, their movements continue in various forms. It seems there is a strong relationship between their organised struggles and the growth in the level and coverage of benefits. Thus, tribal welfare represents essentially a *quid pro quo* in exchange for political quiescence. In sum, the tribal welfare is a much more complex issue than the anthropologists have treated it as a gift of the state for the good of the tribal people. It can neither be separated from the broader historical and social context nor from the implicit ideology. It is primarily biased in favour of surplus appropriating agrarian classes belonging to advanced tribal communities in the form of petty-bourgeois benefits. Such a method of co-operation has not been quite successful for various reasons, and yet, cannot be dispensed away by the state. Meanwhile, the welfare denoting a vague humanitarianism and class conciliation expressed in palliatives, serve as a diversion from the basic social tasks confronting the foiling people, and contribute directly to the reproduction of the system (Pathy, 1982 : 230-47). The innumerable research on welfare have, however, been confined to the official proclamations and judgements.

During the 1950s, several American Anthropologists and foundations, notably the Ford Foundation, spread the message of the community development as the most efficient programme for rural transformation. The striking assumptions of the programme are that it should involve all the households of the village community irrespective of class, caste, creed, and sex; and that the planning and execution should be based on cultural values, norms and traditions of the people. The first assumption, without acknowledging the inherited disparities in the social structure, was instrumental in widening the already existing divisions among the various agrarian classes. It is utopian to think that there would be more or less equal distribution of benefits in the face of dominant landlords and usurers. The second assumption impressed that conflicts can be avoided in the process of social change. Anthropologists did accept the programme uncritically, and before the futility of the programme was realised, the theories of modernisation have already been imported.

The implicit assumptions of modernization are that backwardness is primarily the function of culture and institutional elements; and that, by emulating the western societies, the traditional societies can attain modernization without destroying or modifying the structure. As a result of the acceptance of this irrelevant and outrageously reactionary policy, there has been a massive inflow of finance capital, technology, and knowhow. The proportion of the people below poverty line (more than half) grew rapidly. Unemployment and underemployment grew at the rate of six million per annum. In the name of modernisation, atrocities were and are committed on the peasant and working classes, whenever they raised their just demands. But anthropological studies on modernization remained oblivious of these relations and trends until they were informed by some of their conscientious western colleagues, where they are heading.

The backwardness of India is not due to the cultural reasons, but is the product of the colonial and neo-colonial exploitation and obsolete social relations at home. Development history teaching is accomplished by the decisive and continuous struggles of the oppressed producers to dominate over their product and the conditions of production. It does not necessarily proceed harmoniously or mechanically in a step by step way.

Having considered the major fields of social anthropological interests, let us mention the teaching and other issues. Briefly speaking, the subject matter of social anthropology is confined to social institutions like family kinship, religion, folklore, education, political and economic oranigzations, the units of study like tribe, caste, religious and ethnic communities, urban and rural social groups, etc.; the social processes like co-operation, social control, deviance, integration, diffusion, innovation, communication, socialisation, community development, applied and action anthropology; and a bit of methodology. As a matter of fact, the course contents have very little bearing on the contemporary situation and problems. Fundamental and vital problems like class exploitation and oppression, economic and social justice, discrimination and deprivation, socio-cultural conflicts, expropriation, class collaboration, contradiction and alienation are left out. The students are never encouraged to learn about the social history, methods of struggle and contribution of the people for the development of society. Decisive importance for continuity, and microscopic coverage signifies the role of anthropology as a defender of social conservatism.

While colonial connections are established and understandable, the patron-client relationship flourishing in the post-colonial period is bewildering. Whenever Indian anthropologists have tried to analyse, they have borrowed models, specially from the USA, without any critical attention to their applicability in the Indian context, let alone to its ideological premises. The unproductive aping has lent the subject to near irrelevance. Most borrowed theories are again selective, whose ideology is invariably directed towards system maintenance. The change which is seen from 1960 onwards is basically a replacement of the British scholars by the Americans. Hence, Indian anthropology today is more an Anglo-American legacy than Anglo-Saxon. The advent of support from American foundations, training of Indian anthropologists in U.S. Universities and massive distribution of American anthropological literature at cheap prices produced a whole generation of anthropologists, whose creative thinking has remained insignificant.

Recently, the established anthropologists are facing mounting criticism from some younger scholars. Many of their borrowed theoretical and methodological assumptions have been challenged, and there is fierce controversy about their relevance to the burning problems of the country. This cannot be muted; in fact that powerful chorus of protest is gradually turning into an intellectual influence of creative consequence. Unsparing criticism of all the *status quo* theories and models exposes the ideology of anthropology and the irrelevance of the present research endeavours of the anthropologists. Here lies the seeds of the new; and this is facilitated with the increasing crisis in the society and exposure of the traditional anthropology incapability to comprehend those.

Meanwhile, the anthropologists should shed their value neutrality and stop opposing large scale changes. They need to approach, historically and contextually, large scale regional, national, and international phenomena instead of a 'community', traditional to the discipline. Participant observation and case study methods are not the final methodological judgements in anthropology, and those should not determine the scope of anthropological research. The task is formidable, but let there be attempts to make the subject socially relevant.

## *REFERENCES*

Aguilar, A., 1968. "The Intellectuals and the Revolution," *Monthly Review.*

Pathy, J., 1982. *Agrarian Structure in Tribal Gujarat and Its Implications for Tribal Policies* (mimeo). New Delhi : Indian Council of Social Science Research.

Pathy, J., *et al.* 1976. "Tribal Studies in India : An Appraisal Eastern Anthropologist, 29(4), 399-417.

# 4

# UNDERDEVELOPMENT OF INDIAN SOCIOLOGY

SOCIOLOGY, LIKE all other social sciences, is historically and socially conditioned. It originated in the western milieu to meet primarily the problems which arose in the process of capital accumulation, industrialization and urbanization. For a long time, it continued to reflect only the interests of those societies and the social classes which gave it shape and form. It was thus that Sociology came to be considered a conservative discipline for rationalizing the existing socio-economic order. However, with the passage of time, under changing social conditions, the internal logic of the subject pushed the discipline or part of it beyond the confines of particular classes and societies. In other words, the internal logic of Sociology, combined with the national and social liberation movements, the struggle of the working people, and the dissemination and development of historical and dialectical materialism, played a decisive role in shaping the changing character of conservative Sociology. This process of change in a subject which claims to be the science of human society, through considerably limited and extremely gradual, has made an ever-increasing impact on sociologists round the world.

In India, Sociology is a comparatively late entrant into the academic world. But its origin can be traced back to the days when the British colonial power realized that the knowledge of Indian social life and culture was an essential requirement for the maintenance of its dominance. Since then, it has made a phnoemenal growth and has shown, in the process, sufficient capability to adapt itself to shifts in the socio-political structure.

However, the underdevelopment of Indian Sociology has very much to do with foreign sway over the political economy of the country. This article aims to outline the history of Sociology in India, against the background of its dependence on, and intimate relationship with, one or the other of the imperialist countries. The continuing trends of western ideological elements and their academic and social relevance to Indian society will also be observed.

## COLONIAL SOCIOLOGY

Critics of pre-independence Sociology often characterize it as "colonial Sociology". Such a characterization, though true, ignores a large number of sociological writings which were not only divorced from the colonial interests but critical of colonialism in one way or the other. By overlooking dissent in pre-independence Sociology one fails to account for the internal contradictions of the subject which was grafted on to a totally alien social milieu, and also to recognize the impact of national and other struggles. This does not mean that pre-independence Sociology was to any considerable extent separated from the colonial interest. On the other hand; the critical and committed outlook was manifestly weak, and slow in developing. The major source of underdevelopment of critical and relevant Sociology may be located in the following three factors: (1) its dependence on British Sociology, which had a tardy growth in Britain itself, thus limiting the dynamics of Sociology in India;[1] (2) the difference in the socio-economic conditions in Britain and India restricted the usefulness of the borrowed tools; and, (3) the character of struggles for independence and other causes in India was not particularly conducive to the development of the academic discipline. Thus, the irrelevance of pre-independence Sociology was a product of

1. T. B. Bottomore, "Sociology in India", *The British Journal of Sociology*, vol. XIII, no. 2, June 1962.

socio-academic conditions. But not all that went with Sociology in that period was colonial. It had dissent, in a limited way. Besides, colonial Sociology did not end with the advent of independence. It has continued either as it was, or in modified forms with respect to several aspects of Sociology, even decades after India became independent.

As indicated earlier, the birth of Sociology in India can be traced to the days when colonial authorities realized that the knowledge of Indian tradition and social life was essential for smooth administration. Sociology received much of its impetus from the colonial power. As such it was made to serve the interests of colonialism and its allies, feudalism and bureaucratic capitalism. The British administration encouraged investigation of the village communities and the system of land tenure to facilitate revenue collection. There was studies by Charles Metcalfe (1832), B. H. Baden Powell (1896) and others. Colonialism needed knowledge of Indian culture, and there were scholars like Max-Muller and W.D. Whitney who evinced keen interest in Indology. Various speculative and untenable theories were put forward to account for the origin of castes and their historical development. Meanwhile, the 1871 Census, Imperial and District Gazetteers (1908-09), and All-India Ethnographical Surveys of Castes and Tribes (Nesfield 1885; Risley 1891; Crooke 1896) contained valuable sociological data. There were also studies on the same subject by census officers like Risley, Thurston, O'Malley, Hutton and Guha, and administrators like Dubois (1816), Maine (1861 and 1871) and Fick (1897). During 1910-20, steps were taken to teach Sociology in Indian universities.

Every sociologist was trained to study social organization and religious beliefs and practices. During the 1930s and 1940s, sociologists sought to make contributions to cultural history on the basis of collection and comparison of the customs and values of different castes. However, the bulk of sociological literature included simple descriptive and ethnographical material. The occasional interest to interpret the data was always done with a functional framework uncritically borrowed from Britain.

*Conformists and Dissenters*

In short, sociologists not only helped the British administration by providing information on issues crucial to the British rule, (which was previously the responsibility of untrained administrators, missionaries and tourists) but also other social scientists who "created a high estimate of Indian society, culture and Government. They insisted on a policy of preserving Indian civilization."[2] With a few exceptions almost all the works had exaggerated the segmentary and pluralistic foci of Indian society through the details of castes and tribes and sought to convey that Indian society was never a coherent nation. Emphasis on the continuity of the segmentary society helped the colonial power to implement the policy of "divide and rule".

Hence, "To sum up: the administrative needs of the British rulers led them to collect information about the economic, social and religious life of the people. This task became increasingly complex and systematic as the nineteenth century progressed, and it provided the stimulus for not only social anthropology and Sociology but Indology."[3] In other words, Sociology originated in India in complete isolation from Indian society to buttress colonial interests. And the main body of the literature of the pre-independence period comes to us basically as an imperialist legacy. Hence, one often witnesses extra-academic considerations in the sociological works of that period.

Granting that colonial Sociology was the dominant Sociology in pre-independence days we also notice the contribution of several scholars who were, in their academic pursuits, not only alienated from the colonial interest but also strongly critical of the colonial exploitation. Well-known thinkers like Karl Marx, Henry Marine, C. Bougle and Max Weber had contributed deeper sociological

2. See J. D. Bearce, *British Attitudes towards India*, Oxford 1961, chap. III.

3. M. N. Srinivas and M. N. Panini, "Development of Sociology and Social Anthropology in India", *Sociological Bulletin*, vol. 22, no. 2, September 1973, p. 184.

analyses of Indian village communities, inheritance laws, caste and religion, colonial appropriation, and the possibilities of the emancipation. It is true that although their influence on pre-independence sociologists was marginal, in the post-independence period their works came to be highly valued in the academic circles. Karl Marx's study of the results of British rule in India inspired and reared a whole generation of early Marxists.

Besides, mention also may be made of the influence of Gandhi on several scholars like Nirmal Kumar Bose. There were many like Radhakamal Mukherji, G. L. Ghurye and J. Karve who, in their perspective, supported social reform and tried to incorporate these views in their studies A few Marxist scholars like D. P. Mukherji and Ramkrishna Mukherji analyzed Indian culture and the impact of the British rule quite to the discomfort of the colonial sociologists. D. P. Mukherji who was very critical of empiricism and the intellectual servility of Indian sociologists, said: ' It pains me to observe how our Indian scholars succumb to the lure of modern "scientific' techniques imported from outside as a part of technical aid and 'know-how', without resistance and dignity. In the intellectual transactions which are taking place, it seems that we have no terms to offer, no ground to stand upon."[4] Similar viewpoints may also be noticed among other sociologists of the first generation.

In any case, during the colonial days Sociology largely served the imperial interest and was thus isolated from the Indian society and people. But the socio-economic changes in the country, the national movement, the dissemination of Marxism and the contradictions in the discipline itself allowed a few dissenters who at times stood poles apart from establishment Sociology. This trend, however, could not be developed in the colonial situation beyond a marginal level. Not surprisingly, colonial Sociology did not cease with independence, but made it way straight into the post-independence era.

4. See R. N. Saksena (ed.) *Sociology, Social Research and Social Problems in India*, Asia Publishing House, Bombay 1961, p. 23.

## NEO-COLONIAL SOCIOLOGY

The disintegration of the British Indian empire and achievement of formal political independence do not necessarily mean that colonialism is eliminated. On the contrary, imperialist agencies of America particularly and to a lesser extent Britain continued to subjugate and exploit post-colonial India through such means as unequal trade, arms sales and ideological and political propaganda. Between 1948 and 1960 foreign investments in India more than doubled, growing from Rs. 2558 million to Rs. 5664 million.[5] In a broad sense neo-colonialism is colonialism without empires. It is an indirect system of exploitation of former colonies and semi-colonies. Without going into the details of neo-colonialism in India, this section confines the discussion to Indian Sociology which corresponds to the interests of neo-colonialism: the Sociology which fulfills the requirements of modern imperialist policy, and justifying its operations, helps further realization of its aims.

Following independence the study of Sociology in India has thrived and flourished for a variety of purposes. The new international power, the USA which had already superseded Britain both economically and politically, gradually stated dominating the field. Thus, the change from 1955 onwards has been basically one of replacement of British colonial Sociology by the American neo-colonial variety. This trend became consolidated by the end of 1960s. Before turning to the methods of neo-colonial domination on Indian Sociology and its consequences, it may be necessary to survey in brief the background to the predominance of American influence.

After the Second World War, America emerged as the most powerful country in the world. In order to continue imperialist aggression, increase investment and accumulate profits for its private corporations, it required information about the ex-colonial and semi-colonial countries of Asia, Africa and Latin-America. Consequently, enormous funds were spent for collecting data for the

5. Mathew Kurian, *Impact of Foreign Capital on Indian Economy*, People's Publishing House, New Delhi 1966, pp. 86, 249.

State Department, and "Area Study Programmes" were launched.[6] Besides, it tried to indoctrinate the Third World academics by training them in US universities. financing research, and distributing research, and distributing propaganda literature in glossy academic jackets.

*US Penetration into Universities*

Coming to Indian Sociology in particular, one notice that starting with 1960, several American foundations—Smithsonian, Rockefeller and Ford among them—and PL-480, distributed research funds for both US and Indian scholars (the data collected was often analyzed in the USA and not in India.) provided scholarships and fellowships for training Indian sociologists in US universities, financed establishment of research institutions, and disseminated propaganda literature. The Ford Foundation supported the All India Sociological Society and its conferences.[7] Besides, it is said that one of the Foundation's directors has made "Sociology popular with the Indian Government . . . He played a crucial role in selling the idea of Community Development to the Indian Government."[8] And here it is not necessary to repeat the ideology and the futllity of the Community Development Projects.

As is well known, the funds have well-defined objectives, and are often connected with organizations like the CIA. These are easily evident in the research work carried out with American money. Most, if not all. are simple pieces of apologia for reactionary groups and societies, outside and inside the country. Likewise, the free services of brain-washing in US universities to battalions of Indian students and instructors have comfortably produced a number of Indian sociologists who go on admiring American society, culture and their American mentors.

6. In 1966, a study reported that US anthropologists act as full-time or part-time employees of the CIA or related agencies. See B Nelson, "Anthropologist Debates: Concerns for Future of Foreign Research", *Science*, vol. 154, 1966, p. 525.

7. M. N. Srinivas and M. N. Panini, *op. cit.*, p, 199.

8. *Ibid.*, p. 198.

Anyway, the USA has been successful in its mission in India,[9] as evidenced by the Sociology syllabus in the Indian universities. No less than 60 to 65 per cent of the prescribed readings are from American publications propping up, implicitly and explicitly, neo-colonial interests Similarly, due to American influence a host of conservative concepts and theories have crept into the teaching and research in Sociology. To mention a few, there is frequent use of concepts of hierarchy, adaptation, integration, equilibrium, social control, political socialization, communication, diffusion, innovation and the like, and theories such as functional theory, balance theory, reference group theory and civic culture theories. Invariably, all these are directed towards system maintenance, and tend to act as pillars of the existing dominant classes and societies.

In addition, Indian Sociology follows the lead of reactionary American sociologists like T. Parsons, R. Merton, A. K. Davis, A. F. Bales, H. D. Lasswell, P. F. Lazarsfeed, N. J. Smelser, S. M. Lipset, and G. C. Homans Parsonian jargon and the more recent American cult of statistics are considered the key to the science of society. In the academic world, while it is no sign of ignorance for an Indian student to be unaware of the names of sociologists like Radhakamal Mukherji and D. P. Mukherji, he would be deemed third-rate if unable to use a few esoteric words from Parsons.

Further, a cursory glance at the sociological research in India will easily substantiate the fact that the US has to a great extent reaped its harvest and that the predominant Sociology in India is the neo-colonial version. Overwhelmingly, there is a preoccupation with the study of village community and caste-system. Hence, it may be relevant to elaborate the two important areas of research in post-colonial India.

9. See J. C. Coburn, "Asian Scholars and Government" in Friedman and Seldon (eds ) *America's Asia*, Pantheon, 1971; N. Chomsky, *At War with Asia*, Collins, 1971 and M. Cornoy, *Education as Cultural Imperialism*, David Mckay Co. Inc., New York 1974.

*Village Studies*

Beginning with 1955, several volumes of descriptive, ethnographical and survey-based village monographs were published, for example, Dube (1955, 1958), Majumdar (1955), Marriott (1955), Cohn (1955), Srinivas, *et al.* (1955), Bailey (1957), Lewis (1958), Gould (1960, 1961), Berreman (1962), Wiser (1963), Orenstein (1965), Ishwaran (1967), Gowsami (1967), Vidyarathi (1967) and many more. The essential and representative fact of all these studies is that all hail the functional method of analysis, to a greater or lesser extent. The works are anti-historical, anti-philosophical, mechanistic and positivistic. Very often, generalizations are inducted from an insufficient data from one or two villages, and observations over short periods. Validity of such *ad hoc* and idiosyncratic formulations is open to serious question. Further, due to the restricted vision of impiric sociologists there has been a consistent neglect of the study of persistent and general phenomena. So, even after three decades of village studies, we are not anywhere near a comprehensive theory of systematic understanding of the structure and change in rural India.

Needless to say, all these efforts resulted in providing (though indirectly) some expert counselling to multinational business firms and Government bureaucrats. Partly, this has been done by propagating the idea that modernization and social change in rural India are possible only by adopting modern technology (either imported or related to multinational corporations) and modern outlook. Nothing is said about internal dynamics of village India and the problems of socio-economic dependence. Scientific objectivity is supposed to be attained with the imported structural-functional tools and concepts like diffusion, innovation, adaptation and integration; change is substantiated by a gradual, cumulative accumulation of fluctuation, but not replacement or transformation. Accordingly, during the 1950s and 1960s several sociologists regarded the Community Development Programme as an efficient method for rural transformation.[10] Similarly many things were done in the name of modernization which, in actual practice, came as an intellectual 'aid' from America.

Besides profit, the village studies also sought to maintain order in the Indian rural scene by such superficial and 'pacifying' programmes and also by avoiding any analysis of class-contradictions, which are certain sharp due to unequal distribution of land, the main means of production in the countryside In fact, class is almost always considered unimportant in the anatomy of rural India.

### *Caste Studies*

After independence, caste studies were marked by an emphasis on intensive field-work. They covered functional interdependence of castes, purity and pollution, nature and types of caste mobility, forms of dependence and dominance between castes, and inter-caste frictions. Whatever concepts Indian Sociology has contributed are mainly related to the culture of castes. Srinivas's "Sanskritization" and "Westernization", Dube's "Hierarchical levels of interacting cultural traditions", Marriott's "Universalization" and "Parochialization", and Bailey's "Bridge action", are primarily focused on understanding culture and cultural changes. These concepts are devoid of any scope for the analysis of structural changes (Bailey's is a minor exception). For the structure of castes we have simple descriptive categories like "Dominant caste" of Srinivas, and "Caste, class and power" of Beteille.

Studies on caste-systems and the concepts developed for their analysis take for granted the rationality of the economic system, and are concerned more for values and norms than anything else. So, both village and caste-studies go together in their research framework and ignore the material basis of inequality and the class interests. Caste status is considered most important while

10. See in this context, several papers in A. R. Desai (ed.) *Rural Sociology in India*, The Indian Society of Agricultural Economics, Bombay 1961.

patterns of land distribution and land relations are secondary or tertiary importance. So we have *Caste and the Economic Frontier* (1957), *Caste, Class and Power* (1965), and the like. The importance attached to caste studies is a legacy of colonial Sociology and even now there is no serious move to challenge the unscientific assumptions.

These studies divert attention from the fundamental contradictions and problems in the system, and seek to bring order to a turbulent situation. A leading Indian Sociologist defines the role of the sociologists in India as studying "the principles that govern social life, common living, common sharing of social heritage, and the *continuity of social structure* to guide the course of future of the country whose culture is *eternal*."[11]

Besides, village and caste studies, there are a few works on comparative politics, voting behaviour, socialization, multiple elites, family planning and communication. Invariably all these new fields derived inspiration from American Sociology. Political Sociology pre-supposes that the electoral choice is the locus of politics. Communication Sociology attempts to make the propaganda media effective enough. Industrial Sociology seeks the adaptation of the worker to his work. Likewise are other newly emerging sociological trends in India. All adopt the same structural-functionalist approach.

### *American Shadow*

Recently have come macro-studies of a statistical-positivistic nature undertaken by Saxena. Gore and Desai for the study of votes and attitudes. This cult of statistics is growing. Sociologists like Karve and Beteille follow the Weberian ideal-typical approach in their analysis. There is also a macroscopic philosophical approach which gained a little ground by the propagation of the ideas of L. Dumont who pleaded for combining Sociology with Indology.

11. D. N. Majumdar, "Role of the Sociologists in India," in R. N. Saxena (ed.), *op. cit.*, p. 33.

Functionalists were prompt in condemning the approach[12] because it tends "to revert to Indology . . . (and is) often only a rationalization of traditional customs and institutions."[13] Anyway this approach is adopted by only a few sociologists like Saran.

Notwithstanding the extent of coverage, the boundaries of Indian Sociology remain unclear. Its aims and methods are ill defined and often arbitrary. And we are using such terms as tribe, community, peasant, rural, middle class, plural society, or segmental system, which are extremely imprecise, vague, and insufficiently empirical. Interestingly enough, though India has a number of sociologists, the Government has been asking outside scholars to study its problems: G. Murphy is to study communal problems and even to prepare a textbook on Sociology for Indian students.[14] This speaks volumes not only of Indian sociologists' reputation but also of the state's dependence on western intellectuals.

To sum up the achievements and affirmations of neo-colonial Sociology, being absolutely subservient to American Sociology it has concentrated on trivial and irrelevant problems. Research studies have little bearing on the socio-economic activities of millions of the exploited masses. Basic problems like class oppression, social injustice, expropriation, alienation, and class collaboration are left out of the purview of research. The studies are not at all related to questions of interests, profit, domination and exploitation. In fact, neo-colonial Sociology, with the use of obfuscating jargon and the hypocrisy of objectivity and apoliticism, is organized to produce a mystical, pseudo-reality affirming order in the subcontinent, profit to the multinational corporations, and political hegemony of the United States. Decisive importance to 'values' instead of 'interests' and to continuity instead of change, signifies the role of Sociology as a defender of social conservatism.

12. See the debate in *Contributions to Indian Sociology*, Mouton, Paris, vol. I, 1957; and vol. III, 1959.

13. T. K. N. Unnithan *et al.* (ed.) *Sociology for India*, Prentice Hall of India Pvt. Ltd., New Delhi 1967, p. 5.

14. It was sponsored through UNESCO. T. B. Bottomore, *Sociology A Guide to Literature*, London 1963.

In these circumstances, is there any wonder that Sociology in India is sick and underdeveloped? Is there any historical evidence for the emergence of a genuine discipline anywhere, when it is divorced from the demands of the society with which it should be most concerned?

Change in Sociology after independence is guided by the changing historical forces and bases of structure in India. There has been a shift from British to American Sociology and, interesting to note, not to the German, French, Polish or Soviet varieties. This is not simply because America is the most powerful imperialist country dominating India, but because, unlike other countries, the United States uses Sociology as an instrument for consolidating its aggressive policies. The continuity of British Sociology may be explained from the fact that the relations between colonial and neo-colonial Sociology are not antagonistic. At the same time, because of similar principles of operation, other western powers, albeit to a lesser extent, benefit from neo-colonial Sociology. Soviet Sociology might have made an impact if only it had developed as a social science; its influence, even in the favourable situation of Indo-Soviet cultural relations, remains most limited for this reason. The underdevelopment of Sociology is common to all post-colonial countries where it is well and truly an American import. India is no exception.

## STATE SOCIOLOGY

Considering that a politically independent state has its own problems and interests quite apart from those of the neo-colonialists and that the state in a class society cannot represent the interests of all, it is but natural to manipulate intellectual support for maintaining the edifice of domination. State Sociology is that which directly relates to safeguarding the interests of the state. It is often difficult to distinguish it from neo-colonial Sociology, and from genuine Sociology, as the state under certain socio-historical conditions may appear to enjoy a relative amount of autonomy.

A state has not only to play a repressive role for the maintenance of law and order and accumulation of profit, but also to provide concessions to the common man or at least some sections of the population for creating an ideological and moral support for the establishment. This requires enough information on special issues and propagation of favourable ideas under the cover of Science. Sociology is one field of study wherein to undertake rationalizing and informing the state. For similar ends, business and industrial houses enlist the help of social scientists, giving them well-paid jobs.

The state offers patronage to sociologists through the Research Programmes Committee of the Planning Commission, various ministries, University Grants Commission, Central Social Welfare Board, Indian Council of Social Science Research and similar agencies in the form of research projects. Private capitalists do it through their own research institutes. The project reporters provide facts for planning and administration and highlight some ancillary problems. Repairing the *status quo* is the major concern of a large number of the projects. There are studies on Naxalite movement, Sarvodaya movement, labour disputes, and tribal problems. In return, the researchers for their services to stabilize, consolidate and develop enslavement, are rewarded with status and comfort. The system has immense potentialities to corrupt academics. Only a few succeed in preserving their moorings, while most join the petty-bourgeois rat-race which is speeded up by slanderous fabrications against the class approach, by the use of catchwords like 'national aspirations', 'general welfare', and 'democratic consensus', and if necessary, by criticizing western countries and western Sociology in seminars and classrooms. Even the rhetoric of radicalism is employed to legitimize the reactionary modes of intellectual involvement.[15]

## RELEVANT SOCIOLOGY

The reasons for many sociologists becoming hirelings of the ruling class lie in the socio-class conditions in Indian society, and

15. See K. Marx and F. Engels, *German Ideology*, Progress Publishers, Moscow 1963, pp. 61-72 and A Gramsci, *The Modern Prince and Other Writings*, International Publishers, 1957, pp. 82-83.

the academics' own class background. In fact, Sociology as a profession has contributed to the development of the middle-class point of view in the universities and academic bodies. Sociologists are influenced by the culture and the state of knowledge of the given historical period. The middle-class background makes them vulnerable to adjustment and accommodation to the existing system.

Because of the dominance and patronage of colonial, neo-colonial, and state potentates, a relevant Sociology concerned with the common people of India could not develop. At the same time, the system promoted conformism in a number of ways and remained intolerant of criticism. Yet, there is a small number of Sociologists who find it impossible to turn a blind eye to the existing social contradictions. Some of them were influenced by the sporadic struggles which showed up mass potential for revolutionary action. Since the stimulus from the revolutionary forces is rather limited, a relevant Sociology for the masses is still in an embryonic stage.

Consequently, there are a few scholarly works by D.P. Mukherji, D.D. Kosambi, A.R. Desai, Ramkrishna Mukherji, Kathleen Gough, P.C. Joshi, S. Naqvi, H.P. Sharma, C. Bettelheim, B. Sen, B. Moore, S. A. Dange, Mathew Kurian and others, independent of the clutches of the dominators, and concerned with the people and their inter-relations. The kernel of this type of Sociology is study of the actual life and activities of the social classes in each historical epoch. It is directed at the contradictions in society, its mode of production, as well as superstructure.

Today, this trend is gaining ground because of the growing dissatisfaction with existing Sociology. Some young scholars have started challenging the relevance of borrowed theoretical and methodological assumptions. *Status quo* theories, models and ideology of Sociology, and the irrelevance of present sociological research endeavours are increasingly under mounting criticism. This powerful chorus of protest is gradually turning into an intellectual influence of creative consequence. There is every reason to believe that a genuine Sociology deriving support from Marxism-Leninism holds greater promise for the future transformation of the subject. It is so because Marxism not only generalizes from the tacts but also elaborates its own theory through a critique of the "ideological theoretical practices."[16] However, within the discipline the perspectives are limited and the change will continue to depend on the socio-political struggles, which alone can guide the social orientation of the sociologists and delineate their class identification.

In the light of the foregoing, we may safely conclude that the underdevelopment of Sociology in India is systematically associated with the different forms of domination on Indian political economy over a long period. The social structure of Sociology has been determined by the dominant institutional structure of the society of which Sociology is only a part. It is quite obvious that teaching and research are geared to peace and stability in the turbulence of class society, through counselling the agents of the dominant powers, and disseminating false propaganda in the name of Science. Sociology today is pre-occupied with trivial and irrelevant issues and is exposed to conservative bias. Only when the conditions for the development of a genuine Sociology develop in the country, will it be possible to have a meaningful breakthrough in the subject. [*The author is grateful to Manu Bhaskar and Suguna Paul for their useful comments.*]

16. L. Althusser, *For Marx*, Allen Late, The Penguin Press, 1969, p. 171.

# 5

# POLITICS OF TRIBAL WELFARE : SOME REFLECTIONS

THIS PAPER is neither a review of the available literature on the impact of tribal welfare measures nor is it a review of the various tribal welfare plans and policies. It is rather an unusual attempt at exploration of the ideological basis of the premises of tribal welfare. This demystification is a formidable task not simply because of the absence of relevant literature on the subject but precisely because of the surreptitious use of the welfare policies to subvert the aspirations and struggles of the people. The presentation will be schematic and probably oversimplified. Nonetheless, it is at least, expected to highlight the danger of non-cognition of the politics in tribal welfare.

The central concern of the paper is with the dynamics of the so-called tribal societies and the inherent urge of the state to nip the process in the bud by propagandizing special attention to the 'weaker sections', the Scheduled Tribes in particular, while, attempting to co-opt the dominant sections of the advanced 'tribal' communities and continuing neo-colonial and capitalist domination on the toiling tribal masses. The *ultima ratio* of tribal welfare is rooted in the colonial anthropological perspective of static and homogeneous tribe. This paper tries to expose the myth, and, consequently, evaluates the politics of tribal welfare.

## TRIBAL MOVEMENTS DURING THE RAJ

Little has been systematically written about the colonial exploitation in tribal India and much less, on tribal resistances and struggles. Many still believe that the aborigines are a uniquely mild people unable or unwilling to confront the invaders and exploiters. The scope of this section does not permit us to examine the tribal movements in detail and expose the myth of tribal passivity. The limited purpose is only to suggest that such an obscurantist belief when taken to the axiomatic level, becomes a clear obstacle to the understanding of the relations of the tribes in the wider context and their dynamics.

Anthropologists, whose field until recently, was *de facto* the study of 'primitive' man—the tribe, have portrayed tribal India as static. But the historical evidence proves otherwise. In the past, the non-tribal population of India advanced into the fertile tracts occupied by the tribes, acquired their land by force, and evicted them from their ancestral property. The tribes retreated to hostile and inaccessible areas only after fighting a loosing battle against the mighty outsiders—the kings and the landed gentry. In their resistances to the intrusion of outsiders into their economy, several tribes like the Abor, the Khasi and the Naga could succeed and thus, maintained their cultural identity. It is also evident that the Mughal rulers and Zamindars recognised many tribes like the Bhil, the Gond, the Koli and the Mina as dominant communities. The Gond had their own kingdom—Gondwana. The Deogarh and Kherla dynasties were given independent ruling status during the Mughal regime and were only overthrown by the rise of the Maratha power. Some other tribes like the Binjhal, the Chero, and the Koli had also developed state out of the tribal matrix; and the formation of state stimulated commercial activities, opened trade routes and promoted small scale urbanism (Ghurye, 1963). Of course, in other areas, the powerful kings encouraged the non-tribal people to migrate into tribal pockets so as to facilitate trade and open strategic routes. In turn, the non-tribals enjoyed generous grants of state, mainly in the form of land and protection of rights.

When the British attempted to annex the tribal India, it met with violent opposition. The tribal people were amongst the earliest communities in India who fought against the expansion of colonialism and made the greatest sacrifices. When the British wanted to annex Chhotanagpur, it was strongly opposed in 1780, 1795, 1800, 1801, 1807, 1816 and 1821. Likewise, though the British conquest of Orissa began in 1803, it took 70 to 80 years to bring the Kandhaland under their rule; the Kandha revolted against invasion in 1830, 1835, 1845-54, and 1865-74. But by dint of superior military power and support of the non-tribal people, the British brought most of the tribal region under its control. And where it failed to suppress the revolts, the concept of protection developed in stages. The earliest mode of protective administration was the Agency system, aimed at quelling rebellions. But whenever the movements were cooled down, the draconian jaws of colonial exploitation were extended.

The tribal regions of Bihar, Bengal, Western Orissa and eastern parts of Central Provinces were brought under the Zamindari system, and those of Bombay, Gujarat and Western parts of Central Provinces to the ryotwari system. Tribal chiefs, muthaheads, kings and non-tribal merchants, and landlords were recognised as Zamindars/malgujars. The colonial power was keen on extending cultivation of waste lands to increase its revenue and as often the tribal land was found ownerless, it was handed over to landlords who promised to pay the rent. In this way, large tracts of tribal land passed from aboriginal ownership to non-tribal Zamindars reducing the real owners to tenants and casual labourers (Fuchs, 1960).

The colonial system strengthened both the feudal crust of tribal and non-tribal society, and simultaneously created conditions for the growth of rampaging market forces. Many people were forced and some opted to take up commodity production on a limited scale. Cash crops like cotton, jute, sugarcane, turmeric, tobacco and opium were produced, and forest produces like lac were collected for the market. Besides, colonialism created a demand for money in the tribal economy to pay land revenue, plough tax, cess tax and other levies. Home brewing was denied and excise duty was collected. The forest got reserved. All these changes brought the outside landlords, merchants, money-lenders, *Amlas* into their midst. Their best lands were taken by them. The peasants got indebted giving birth to obnoxious system of slavery. Besides the forcible extraction of *begar*, the roads, bridges and even schools were constructed with the *bheti*.

At the same time, large tea, coffee and rubber estates were created in Assam and south Indian hills by dispossessing the tribal population and forcing them to work as plantation labourers. Pace of immigration to plantations and mines rose phenomenally; for instance, between 1891 and 1921 in Chhotanagpur alone, the incidence of outmigration rose from 3,30,000 to 9,47,000. Besides the Kol and other tribes were forced with overseas migration as labourers, mainly to Mauritius. Between 1840-1870, the figure reached 55,000. Many tribes like the Bhil were recruited into the military in large numbers. And in 1917, several thousands of the Kandha were taken to Mesopotamia to serve in World War I.

In short, colonialism helped in breaking down the remaining communal mode of production and created private property in land; implanted traditional tribal leadership and the outside landlords as the owners of the land—turning the actual tillers into tenants or labourers; introduced money economy in the form of numerous taxes and cash crop production; merchants, traders and peddlers were allowed to settle down in the region and received protection; and, forcibly recruited people for plantations, mines and army, both inside and outside the country. In other words, it instituted policies of paternalism and repression that sought to ensure a steady and reliable work-force and raw materials, and also maintenance of the *status quo* of its allies—the tribal and non-tribal landlords, mainly the latter, and the usurers. All this has been done in the name of 'indirect rule'. The piratical plunder of resources, forced labour, deportations and massacres were justified through the notorious 'White Man's Burden' ideology.

To ensure this, colonialism attempted to divide the tribes, by pointing out and exaggerating those factors which separated them so as to lessen the chances of unity among these groups; and secondly, by removing a few rich 'assimilated' persons into the colonial framework thus encouraging individual aspirations. Attempts were made to indoctrinate through the churches. The Christian missionaries and evangelists rationalised the British rule, and sought to create a new bastion of support from among the tribal people. These attempts at division, however, heightened ethnic consciousness and later, stimulated the militant agitations against feudal and colonial aggressions.

Unlike the belief in tribal apathy, most of the settled agricultural tribes fought against exploitation by outsiders. It is true that land alienation—the crucial issue of the movements—was not only between tribe *Vs.* non-tribe but also within and in-between tribal communities. But the intra-tribal contradictions were overshadowed by the onslaught of non-tribals; and, the bonds of kinship, ethnicity and tradition spared their own exploiting people from attack. In fact, initially, the movements were led by their chiefs who were partially or totally deprived of their traditional rights.

Let us briefly mention a few movements of some tribes during colonial period and see their general character. The Santhal, the second largest tribal community in India, rose in revolt against rapecious landlords, money-lenders and the colonial exploiters in 1855, 1871 and 1885, and supported national movement towards the middle of 1930s. The Munda fought against the same intruders in 1789, 1808, 1811, 1818, 1820, 1832, 1857, 1887-90 and 1895-97. The Oraon, now demanding a Jharkhand state, took up arms against the British in 1895-97, 1915 and 1918 and participated in non-co-operation movement in 19-0. The Koya of Andhra Pradesh revolted against the *Muttadars*, who enforced *Vetti* and took away their best lands, in 1809, 1862 and 1879. In 1831-32, the Kol rebelled against the settlement of their land with outsiders, arbitrary enhancement of rent, and forcible extraction of labour. The Gond and the Kolam of Andhra Pradesh protested against land alienation and forest reservation rules in 1941-43. Still, there were many more movements in different parts of tribal India (Mohapatra, 1972; Commissioner of Scheduled Areas and Scheduled Tribes, Govt. of India, 1960-61 : 3-24).

The striking features of these movements were that the tribes most involved were numerically strong and settled agriculturalists. Secondly, the major causes of their struggle were land alienation, land grant to contractors and army officials, heavy taxation of land, forced labour including forcible recruitment to plantations, mines and army, and reservation of forest. The additional factors were excise policy, use of force to cultivate cash crops, loss of independence, culture and religion. The significant issue, however, was connected with land. Thirdly, the movements were directed against alien Zamindars, contractors, revenue collectors, British domination and Christian missionaries. Many movements towards the end, like that of the Munda, the Oraon, the Koya, and the Gond became explicitly anti-colonial, though without a sustained ideology of nationalism. Rand Guidallo, Tantiya Bhil, Vishnu Gond, Birsa Munda, Surendra Sai, Kangla Manjhi, Kanu and Siddhu Murmu *et al* were the great freedom fighters. Fourthly, the movements started with ethnic overtones where the main slogan was that non-tribals should be ousted from the tribal territory. This covered the internal exploitation by their own people. Fifthly, and the most important of all is that the movements were invariably agrarian and defensive. They were violent in their means (exceptions apart) and political in their ends (Gough, 1974). Lastly, all the movements were crushed with the military might of colonialism. Cold-blooded murder, execution, burning dow villages and fields, arrest and intimidation were the common follow ups. Ex-servicemen were settled in the 'troubled' regions. Criminal Tribes Act was promulgated, the Zamindars—both local and outsider—were entrusted with the management of police force (Siddiqui, 1976). At the same time, piece-meal reforms in the form of reduction of rent, administrative and legal concessions like Santhal Pargana Regulation (1873), Chhotanagpur Tenancy Act (1908). Central Provinces Legislation (1916), etc. and instalment of some traditional tribal chiefs into the positions of power were carried out. But the solution was nowhere near, fires continued to blaze underneath the 'peaceful' situation.

Mass movements of the tribal people against colonialism and feudalism are often reduced by the colonial scholars to the mobilization of tribes for patronage. This is absurd caricature of the political struggles of the toiling and democratic masses drawn from varied tribes and castes. This does not mean that there were no reformative or emulative movements, but those were all short-lived and had no enduring impact on the people (Sharma, 1976). There were a number of weaknesses in the movements. But the point is that the advanced tribal communities were never passive to their exploitation, repeatedly they revolted against much a mighty colonial power and that cannot but have bearing in the formulation of tribal policies in independent India.

## INTERNAL DIFFERENTIATION AND CO-OPTION

With the attainment of independence, the architects of the Constitution of India recognized the importance of various militant agrarian movements in tribal India during the colonial period, and attempts were made to avoid such occurrences in future. What Ambedkar spoke in the Constituent Assembly on the 25th November, 1949, deserves mention here. He said :

> On the 26th January, 1950, we are going to enter into a life of contradictions. In politics we will have equality and in social economic life we will have inequality .. How long shall we continue to deny equality in our social and economic life ?. . . We must remove this contradiction at the earliest possible moment or else those who suffer from inequality will blow up the structure of political democracy (cited in Rao, 1868 : 944-945).

And almost after a quarter century, the Commissioner for Scheduled Castes and Scheduled Tribes repeats the warning in a more explicit way :

> History is a witness that even the poor, however helpless and powerless they may be, cannot go on submitting to the high-handedness and oppression of the upper strata of society for all times to come; and time does come when they themselves wake up to shake off the shackles of poverty, helplessness and

misery in whatever way they find it possible, such a situation can lead to undesirable consequences too, and *we have to avoid it as far as possible in the interest of the nation, its integrity, its development, its prosperity* (1971-72 and 1972-73 : 6, emphasis added).

The state knows very well that out of the 414 different Scheduled Tribes, only some 20 to 30 tribal communities are dangerous to the establishment. And they only had repeatedly challenged the colonial administration in the past. Others, being small and undifferentiated cannot launch effective struggles to achieve rightful place with the larger multinational state. Thus, the problem is how to 'assimilate' the bigger tribes? Two ways are open for that : one, the use of outright brutal force. and the other, the accommodation of their dominant classes into the equivalent positions in the broader state. with some political and ideological concessions. But, in a parliamentary democracy much cannot be relied on the first method. hence ultimately the importance is given to the second alternative. Nevertheless, the second method is possible only when the dominant classes of the advanced tribal communities acknowledge that neither they can struggle nor can compete with the ruling classes of the state. In due course, however, the dominant classes of tribal communities confront a deteriorating position and get either co-opted with the ruling class as a subordinate ally or forced close to the fold of subject class(es). The process of integration is accelerated with the development of capitalism (Pathy, 1978).

In brief, the strategy opted is to co-opt the dominant classes of the advanced tribal communities so as to avoid the 'undesirable consequences'. But the fact, that in India, there exist different pre-capitalist modes of production and capitalism is weak and dependent, *in se* means that even when a few are co-opted, it does not necessarily assimilate the communities as a whole, is being ignored.

Anyhow, the ideology of co-option to intercept anticipated agrarian and sub-national struggles of the tribal masses is never made open. The camouflaging is carried out on humanitarian grounds under the cover of democratic responsibility and intellectual veneer. In this connection, the notions of the colonial tribal anthropology are used as the *ratio aqendi*.

The *notiones communes* with regard to the tribes are that because of their unique historical and cultural setting, they remain backward in comparison to the non-tribal population of India and represent a 'cultural lag'. They are small, self-contained, self-sufficient, autonomous communities practising subsistence economy with the lack of or limited external trade. Thus, they are homogeneous and unstructured units of production and consumption, devoid of any exploitation and social conflict. Accordingly, every tribal more or less equally benefits from a given policy and expenditure of the state extended towards these communities. Besides, there is a sharp dichotomy between tribals and non-tribals, the latter being the exploiter of the former (Paul and Bhasker, 1976). The 'value-free' scholars have shown strong reluctance to believe in the existence of unequal distribution of land, emergence and development of exploitative groups based on antagonistic relations of production characterised by extensive social division of labour *within* the tribal societies.

These notions, particularly that the tribes are unstructured, meant that these privileges and protective measures guaranteed through Article 46 and other 18 articles and two special Schedules would naturally benefit the tribal people *en bloc*. This appears to be the crux of the strategy of tribal co-option. Thus, the myth needs a little elaborate exposition.

The 414 officially recognised tribal communities show strikingly enormous diversity among them. A number of small tribes like the Chenchu, the Irula, the Jarawa, the Kadar, the Shompen live by hunting and gathering. Their numerical strength does not perhaps exceed a few thousands. But, approximately 2.6 millions of tribals belonging to various tribes depend upon slash and burn cultivation over an annual area of about 1.4 million acres (Table 1). Generally shifting land belong to the village and is common property of the lineage. Among some of the tribes like the Angami Naga. The Ao Naga, and the Garo, land is held jointly by the clan having more or less established permanent politico-juridical authority, wherein the leadership gets extra-economic privileges over and above other members. For the sake of simplicity, let us assume that all those who practice hunting, gathering, and shifting cultivation, do not have internal differentiation, and they are homogeneous and unstructured. When the help of the state is extended to them, that may more or less equally benefit all. But their strength to the total tribal population is not more than 10 per cent. Mention may be made here that some non-tribals in tribal belts do live by slash-and-burn cultivation, though by official definition they are also exploiters of tribals.

There are a few pastoral communities like the Bakarwal and the Gaddi, who also practice agriculture and participate in local market. They have differences in ownership of animals, land, and use of labour. Their strength too is no more than a few thousands. There are also about 4.5 per cent of the tribal population belonging to different tribes engaged in non-agricultural sector—plantations, mines, industries—as labourers.

But the bigger tribal communities like the Bhil, the Bhuiya, the Binjhal, the Gond, the Ho, the Kandha, the Koli, the Koya, the Mina, the Munda, several Nagas, the Oraon, and the Santhal had tribal aristocracy and warrior nobility who in due course with economic privileges, gifts, rents, use of 'free' and slave labour got more surplus and got themselves separated from the labour process. These communities comprise three-fourth of the total tribal population. They have already developed *class* structure. There are landlords, serfs or tenants in each of these communities. In some communities, there are even culturally correlated categories. The Munda has three sections—Bhumij Mundas are the landlords, ordinary Mundas are the peasants, and Khangar Mundas are the serfs or labourers. Among the Sherdukpen, there are the Thongs who are the landowning classes and Chhaos are the serfs. Similarly, the Baiga has two divisions, Binjhwar and ordinary Baiga; the Korku has Muwasis and Patharies and Bhilala has Bara Bhilala and Barelas; the Gond has Raj Gond, Dhur Gond and Kamis; and so on. Often, the smaller tribes serve the dominant classes of these advanced tribes, for instance, to the Raj Gonds, the Ahir, the Ghasi, the Kaller and the Pradhan serve in different ways. Besides, it is not uncommon to witness non-tribal working in the field of tribal landlords and rich peasants.

A comparison between the pattern of land distribution among the Scheduled Tribes and the general population (which also include the STs) reveals several interesting features (Table 2): (1) among the cultivators in India the percentage of households owning less than 2.5 acres of land is considerably higher than among the tribal households, while the percentage of holding above 2.5 acres is higher in case of tribals than the all-India percentage, except with a minor difference in Kerala, Mysore and Rajasthan; and, (2) about 10.62 per cent of tribal households own more than 15 acres of land when 54.71 per cent of the tribals own less than 5 acres each. If the first observation has to be qualified with overall low productivity of land in the tribal region, the second remains significant for the present purpose, in that when 85 per cent of the tribals are agriculturists, the disparities in landholding alone demonstrate the existence of different classes within the tribal societies.

Instances are also not uncommon that the big tribal landlords employ bonded or contract labour for cultivation. They also participate in money-lending. In a study conducted in a tribal village of Andhra Pradesh during 1969-70, it was revealed that 61.24 per cent of the households in the village were indebted. The incidence was high among the landless households. Among the cultivators, the percentage of indebted households declined as the size of holdings increased. About 80 per cent of the total credit requirements of the tribal borrowers were met by rich tribals (cited in, Commissioner for SCs and STs, 1971-72, and 1972-73 : 213). Similarly, another study in Orissa revealed that 66.7 per cent of households were indebted in 1971. Further, 36.9 per cent of the total loan was taken from tribal money-lenders (Commissioner for SCs and STs 1972-73 : 213-14; Pathy, 1976A : 23-24). This does not mean that the non-tribal money-lenders, are less important; it only means that there are tribal money-lenders, and the money-lending has created bondage of the tribal people in the form of Vetti, Gothi, Hali, Jeetha, Sagri, Begar, Mat, Sanjayat, etc.

In short, excluding a-tenth of the total tribal population, the rest have developed internal differentiation and class structures. There are contradictions between and within them. By this, the domination of non-tribals is not ignored; the argument only refers that there are tribal exploiters who exploit the tribal labour as well as non-tribal poor; and that all non-tribals are not exploiters of the tribal people, only those non-tribals who have established economic dominance in the area, exploit the tribes who are the have-nots in their own locality (Pathy, *et al*, 1976B).

Anyway, the *nervus probandi* is that when the major tribal communities are structured, logically the indiscriminate extension of benefits would go to the upper strata of the population, who own more land and have the benefit of either traditional political institutions or the modern political structure. It is utopian to think that in an exploitative society, there would be more or less equal distribution of benefits. A reference to protection is a necessary reference to the protection of the status quo of exploitation in the tribal villages Similarly, the extension of political, administrative and economic concessions cannot but strengthen the existing domination or create an 'elite' isolated from the tribal structure itself. Some studies have indeed noticed that state help has reached only to a minor section of tribals who in fact got separated from the parental way of life. No wonder, that their fellow tribesmen regard them as *dikku*, i.e., robbers (Sachhidananda, 1964).

That is indeed what the state requires for its strategy to subvert agrarian and sub-nationalist struggles. And there are a few scholars who agree with it and openly argue that 'a strategy of nation-building will, in some context, require that the rate of advancement of the advanced sections among the tribals should be accelerated so that the process of creation of one national elite is completed. This is indispensable for reducing the inter-ethnic distances within the national policy' (Roy Burman, 1975 : 52). Such an argument fails to see that the emergence of the tribal rich takes place not only with the state's expenditure but also at the cost of the toiling tribal population; and that, being a late comer, the tribal 'elite' cannot compete in equal terms with the other 'elites'.

A glance at the welfare policies would further lend support to the position taken above. Almost all states provide protection to Scheduled Tribes against alienation of their land (Murdia, 1975). But there is no legislation for alienation of land by the *tribal* rich of the advanced tribal societies. In Meghalaya, outside tribals such as Mizos are buying land from the poor Khasi people (Commissioner for SCs and STs 1971-72 and 1972-73 : 184-185). In Manipur, the tribal chiefs have sold considerable amount of land to outsiders, mostly to the Gorkhas. However, with the defective legislations and coercion or fraud by non-tribal rich, the illegal transactions continue unabated—which is nothing surprising considering the dominant position of the rich non-tribals in the state and society.

In education, not only seats are reserved in technical institutes and scholarships are instituted but also scholarships are awarded to the Scheduled Tribes for post graduate research abroad. In the field of all India services, reservation are there for Scheduled Tribes. In 1972, Scheduled Tribes constituted 3.11 per cent of IAS and 1.75 per cent of IPS. Similarly, Articles 330, 332 and 334 provide for reservation of seats for Scheduled Tribes in the Parliament and State Assemblies. Interestingly, they hardly return from non-reserved constituencies. An analysis of the background of tribal MPs in 1971 revealed that 22.9 per cent had urban background and 37.1 per cent had college or University degrees including professional course, and 2.9 per cent had business industry as occupation (Narayana, 1978). In Orissa, the tribal MLAs of 1974 belonged to six major tribes (out of sixty two) and about 80 per cent of them belonged to large landowning groups (Pathy, 1977) Now the question is that who could enjoy the reservation and other privileges for such prestigeous intellectual, bureaucratic and political positions; and, after getting them how could they adjust with their 'backward, static and homogeneous' societies. One can rationalize the policies if one subscribes to the aim of the state for 'reducing inter-ethnic distances'.

Naturally, with the kind of tribal welfare activities going on over the arch reactionary premises, one cannot but tend to believe that there may be some political connotations in the formulation, notably the ethnic co-option to avoid the struggles and also to divert the attention of non-tribals from the fundamental problems of the society. This is particularly so, when three-fifth of the population remains below the 'poverty line', attention to Scheduled Castes and Scheduled Tribes constituting only a fifth, is to safeguard the moribund system while picking up the fellow class people from among the 'weaker sections'.

So far, the discussion has remained confined to the ideology of tribal welfare, with an occasional reference to non-tribal exploitation. But there is also the issue of the domination of the state, and neo-colonialism on tribal India. This further warrants the need to cultivate the present welfare policy. The state procures the excise revenue through its contractors. The forest is reserved in the interest of the nation and its environment and several industries, financed by multinational corporations and capitalist countries, are set up in the midst of tribal region. Rourkella, Ranchi, Bailadila, Kiruburu and others have to flourish over the tribal land and cheap labour, profiting the financial tycoons and the state. Hardly they are rehabilitated. Table 4 shows that only 38.64 per cent of the displaced families are rehabilitated and that they were allotted 10.94 per cent of their previous land holdings. On the whole, the question of neo-colonial domination over tribal India is a vital area of investigation for understanding both the complexity of ideology of tribal welfare and the tribal struggles.

## EPILOGUE

To recapitulate the foregoing, the romantic picture of the tribes conveys that they are homogeneous and static units, and that they are empirically closed. But *in concreto*, they have extensions in, and interactions with the outside world both in time and space. Mostly, they have an internal class structure and are dynamic. The intellectual default has in a sense shaped the officially organised welfare work in tribal India

The tribal welfare is geared, firstly to subvert the anticipated struggles in the tribal belts through co-opting the feudal classes of the advanced tribal societies and creating an alienated elite from among them and, secondly, to divert the attention of the millions of the oppressed people of India by implicitly propogandizing the myth that they are well off than the tribal people—probably including the erstwhile tribal kings, chiefs and Zamindars, and also the present tribal MLAs, MPs, IAS officers, foreign returned post-graduates and the like.

But because of the weakness of capitalism in India, ethnic loyalties continue to exist. The strategy of inhibiting the movements by ethnic co-option seems to be a failure, or at least tending towards that.

The situation created by colonialism does more or less persist in tribal India. People face the same problems and even more with regard to land, forest and labour. Tribal India is restless. The revolts of the Naga and the Mizo are too well known to be recounted here. The Ahom, the Khasi, the Oraon, and others are filled with a new sub-nationality consciousness. There are movements by the Bhil, the Bhutia, the Gond, the Jatapu, the Kandha, the Kolam, and the Saora, Naxalite movement, Jharkhand movement, and Bhoomi Sena movement are just a few to note here. The struggles are invariably due to land alienation, enhancement of rent, compulsory labour, encroachment on forest rights, low wages, and expansion of industries without adequate compensation. They are crushed with the powerful army. Notwithstanding the great concern for the tribal people, the repression is no less severe than what the British did. But the movements continue to appear everywhere, and it is not going to be easy to prevent or obstruct their occurrence with the present strategy.

NOTE—The readers would do well to see S. C. Varma's brilliant and incisive analysis of the Hindi film, *Akrosh* (EA 34 : 4, 1981), which makes an excellent corroborative reading on the basic theme and contention of this paper.

Table 1

*Tribal Population Practising Shifting Cultivation and the Acreage*

| *State* | *Name of the Tribes* | *Population* | *Acreage utilised annually* |
|---|---|---|---|
| Andhra Pradesh | Gadaba, Kotiya, Koya, Mali, Nayak | 2,00,000 | 96,000 |
| Assam | Chakma, Care, Lushai, Mikir | 9,79,000 | 5,08,800 |
| Bihar | Kharia, Korwa, Mal-paharia | 1,15,000 | 436 |
| Gujarat | Kubbi, Kokany, Mavichi | 25.000 | 72,300 |
| Kerala | Irula, Kurumba, Mudugar | 10,000 | 54,000 |
| M.P. | Baiga, Bharia | 30,000 | 44,000 |
| Madras | Kadar, Kurumba, Malasar | 2,200 | 3.200 |
| Mysore | Kumbi, Kumari, Soligar | 14.000 | 2,500 |
| Orissa | Jatapur, Juang, Koya, Kutia, Kandha | 9,35,700 | 4,00,000 |
| Manipur | Angami, Maring, Tangkhed | 1,83,000 | 54,C00 |
| Tripura | Halam, Kuki, Mag, Noatia | 95,501 | 1,16,900 |
| Total | | 25,89,401 | 13,51,936 |

*Source :* *Report*, Commissioner of Scheduled Areas and Scheduled Tribes, 1961-62, New Delhi, pp. 144-45.

*Note :* (1) Neither all the tribes practising shifting cultivation are mentioned nor all those mentioned the total population depend on shifting agriculture alone.

(2) Figures are though approximate, it is likely that they might have been reduced in the last 18 years.

**Table 2**

*Statewise Percentage of Households (All Communities and Tribes) in Cultivation Classified by Size of Land Cultivated*

| State | Less than 2.5 acres | | 2.5 to 5 acres | | 5 to 10 acres | | 10 to 15 acres | | above 15 acres | |
|---|---|---|---|---|---|---|---|---|---|---|
| | All Comm. | Tribal | All Comm. | Tribal | All Comm. | Tribal | All Comm. | Tribal | All Comm. | Tribal |
| Andhra Pradesh | 69.25 | 34.94 | 11.15 | 22.26 | 11.15 | 22.81 | 4.52 | 10.82 | 7.23 | 9.17 |
| Assam | 60.82 | 29 78 | 24.01 | 34.74 | 12 85 | 24.37 | 1.73 | 5.88 | 0.59 | 5.13 |
| Bihar | 65.17 | 36.56 | 17.69 | 30.61 | 11.29 | 22.23 | 3.44 | 6 16 | 2.60 | 4.44 |
| Gujarat | 47.09 | 25 55 | 11.59 | 25.98 | 16.17 | 28 41 | 9.49 | 10.46 | 15.66 | 9.55 |
| Kerala | 85.19 | 53.30 | 8.75 | 25.58 | 4.25 | 16.28 | 1.09 | 3.67 | 0.72 | 1.17 |
| Madhya Pradesh | 39.20 | 16.76 | 15.63 | 19 06 | 20 33 | 29.32 | 10.26 | 16.13 | 14.58 | 18.74 |
| Maharashtra | 48.60 | 19.63 | 12.40 | 18 51 | 14 10 | 24 86 | 8.34 | 14.25 | 16.56 | 22.75 |
| Mysore | 43.99 | 38 05 | 13.23 | 21.01 | 21.28 | 19.15 | 8.72 | 11.17 | 12.78 | 10.62 |
| Orissa | 59.70 | 37.13 | 19.24 | 26.86 | 13.48 | 22.65 | 4.50 | 7.10 | 3.08 | 6.26 |
| Rajasthan | 26.89 | 21.80 | 16.58 | 24.41 | 21.62 | 27.90 | 11.50 | 11.64 | 23.41 | 14.25 |
| Tamil Nadu | 75.07 | 35.42 | 12.94 | 33.21 | 8.44 | 23.28 | 2.20 | 4.99 | 1.35 | 3.10 |
| West Bengal | 63.57 | 44.85 | 19.62 | 29.08 | 12.31 | 19.55 | 3.42 | 3.92 | 1.08 | 2.60 |

***Sources*** **:** (i) V. M. Dandekar and Nilakantha Rath, 'Poverty in India—II : Policies and Programmes', *Economic and Political Weekly*, Volume, VI (1971), No. 2, 110-111.

(ii) ***Report***, Commissioner for Scheduled Caste and Scheduled Tribes, 1966-67, pp, 116-117.

Table 3

*Tribal Families Displaced, Rehabilitated and the Land Allotted as Compensation, 1968-73*

| *Year* | *Displaced family* | *Displaced from Acreage* | *Rehabilitated families* | *Allotted acreage* |
|---|---|---|---|---|
| 1968-69* | 817 | 5,877 | 309 | — |
| 1969-70* | 2,399 | 20,095 | 1,412 | 2,036 |
| 1970-71* | 40 | 103 | 18 | 28 |
| 1971-72** | 4,561 | 21,199 | 1,587 | 3,959 |
| 1972-73* | 2,310 | 10,550 | 590 | 305 |
| Total | 10,127 | 57,834 | 3,916 | 6,328 |

*Notes* : * Information available for Gujarat, Kerala, M.P., Maharashtra, Rajasthan, Tamil Nadu, West Bengal and Himachal Pradesh.

** Information available for Maharashtra, Manipur, West Bengal and Rajasthan only.

*Source* : *Report*, Commissioner for Scheduled Castes and Scheduled Tribes, 1971-1972 and 1972-73, pp. 190-191.

## *REFERENCES*

Fuchs, S., 1960. *The Gond and Bhumia of Eastern Mandla*, Bombay.

Ghuryo, G. S., 1963. *The Scheduled Tribes*. Bombay : Popular Prakashan.

Gough, Kathleen, 1974. 'Indian Peasant Uprisings', *Economic and Political Weekly*, Special No., 1391-1412.

Government of India, 1960-61. *Report, Commissioner for the Scheduled Areas and Scheduled Tribes*, Vol. 1.

——, 1971-72 & 1972-73. *Report, Commissioner for the Scheduled Castes and Scheduled Tribes.*

Mohapatra, L. K., 1972. 'Social Movements among Tribes in India', in K. Suresh Singh (ed.), *Tribal Situation in India*. Simla : Indian Institute of Advanced Study.

Murdia, Ratna, 1975. 'Land Allotment and Land Alienation: Policies and Programmes for Scheduled Castes and Scheduled Tribes', *Economic and Political Weekly*, Vol. 10, No. 32, pp. 1204-14.

Narayana, G., 1978. 'Social Background of Scheduled Caste Lok Sabha Members, 1962-1971'. *Economic and Political Weekly*, Vol. XIII, No. 37, 1603-1608.

Pathy, J., 1976a. 'Political Economy of Kandhaland' *Man in India*, Vol. 56 (1976A). No. 1, 1-36.

——, 1973b. *et. al.* 'Tribal Studies in India: An Appraisal', *The Eastern Anthropologist*, Vol. 29, (1975B) No. 4, 401-17.

——, 1977. Political Elite of Orissa', Ph. D. dissertation. New Delhi: Jawaharlal Nehru University.

——, 1978. 'An Outline of Modes of Production in Tribal India', paper presented in 5th All India Conference of the Indian School of Social Sciences, Calcutta, Jan., 21 23.

Paul, S. and Manu Bhaskar, 1976. 'Indian Tribes: Illusion and Reality', *The Sunday Statesman Magazine*, Dec. 5.

Rao, B. Shiva, 1968. *The Framing of India's Constitution: Select Documents*. New Delhi: Indian Institute of Public Administration, Vol. IV.

Roy Burman, B.K., 1975. 'Perspectives for Administration and Development of the Scheduled Tribes', in V.R.K. Paramahamsa (ed.), *Perspectives on Tribal Development and Administration*'. Hyderabad: National Institute of Community Development.

Sachchidananda, 1964. *Culture Change in Tribal Bihar: Munda and Oraon*. Calcutta.

Sharma, K. L., 1976. 'Jharkhand Movement in Bihar', *Economic and Political Weekly*, Vol. XI, Nos. 1-2, 37-43.

Siddiqui, M. H., 1976. 'Colonialism and Tribal Social Structure: Chota Nagpur: 1772-1900', Paper for UNESCO Conference on *Trends in Ethnic Group Relations in Asia*. Manila, March 8-12.

# 6

# LAND REFORMS IN INDIA : IMPERATIVES AND POTENTIALS

LAND REFORMS have been repeatedly hailed as harbingers of socialism in India. However, experience over a quarter century strongly refutes the claim. Land reforms were carried out not simply as a question of social justice or to ameliorate the living conditions of the rural poor, but rather, *due to the crying need of the Indian industry.* A highly inquitous and skewed pattern of landholding constitutes a barrier not only for agricultural production but also to industrial growth by limiting the market for industrial goods. Feudal relations with various forms of tenancy, permanent labour, excessive importance of land rent, food loans to workers at exorbitant rates on enslaving terms, payment of wages in kind, widespread extra-economic compulsions, personal subservience of the immediate producer to the landlords and the like, are naturally a great hindrance to the growth of a home market. Consequently, normal development of commodity, production and industrial development are inhibited. Thus, land reforms are considered essential for the development of the home market, which alone can stimulate Indian industry.

Precisely for the same reason, the Indian capitalists have been among the strongest advocates of land reforms. As early as June 28, 1946, The *Eastern Economist* controlled by the Birla House wrote of the necessity of "bringing into the service of agriculture a very much larger share of the organizing ability and capital of the community, than it has received so far," and declared that the

Zamindar "has no economic justification for his existence". Likewise, the Indian National Congress since at least the Karachi Resolution (1931), considered the urgency of land reforms so as to accelerate the pace of capitalist development. These reforms were to be accomplished by legislations within the context of the democratic political system and with due respect for existing property rights.

Following Independence, through the legislative means, the zamindari and jagirdari tenures were more or less successfully abolished within a decade. Although substantial compensations were paid to the intermediaries, the Government did succeed perceptably in curbing the domination of some of the princes and absentee landlords, and eliminating many a feudal form of oppression and extortion from which the tenants of the erstwhile intermediaries suffered. The abolition of intermediary tenures was possible. On the one hand the parasitic class of landlords were ideologically and morally alienated on account of their identification with colonialism. On the other we had the States' requirement of more land revenue—which, incidentally, was a paltry sum in the Zamindari areas, and the need of the business class to profitably exploit industrial raw materials, which existed in abundance in those estates. Simultaneously, the process got precipitated by the necessity of the State to mollify peasant movements in different parts of the country.

Nonetheless, the abolition of intermediary tenures, the major anti-feudal reform to date, did not produce any radical change in property relations. It was largely a reform of revenue administration rather than a measure of redistribution of land to the tiller. The intermediaries have also retained much of the cultivable land as they were helped through legal exemptions by both legislature and bureaucracy, where they had disproportionate dominance. Besides, as in many parts, the Zamindars alone had their land records, they simply manipulated and transferred in favour of near and far relatives, servants, priests and temples, before handing over the records to the respective authorities. Also, to deflate the revenue, they have recorded a sizable portion as non-agriculture land. This was later used to evade ceiling legislations.

The next important exercise was fixing ceilings on landownership, and distribution of the surplus land to the small peasants and landless labourers, with special preference to the backward communities. Prior to that the states had tried to persuade the die-hard landlords to voluntarily surrender their surplus land as a philanthropic gesture. But that failed to cut much ice. And hence, with ample warning, ceiling laws were enacted. The very influence of the landlords in the legislatures ensured having enough built in loopholes so that the provisions could not be enforced. Legally, innumerable exemptions are given for pasture, garden, efficiently managed farms, commercial cropping, factory sites, religious institutions and the like. This in essence resulted in the forceful eviction of tenants and small peasants, persistence of excessive concentration of land, rise in the number of agricultural labourers and keeping the rural society in excruciating moral pain.

In the 16 Indian States which implemented land ceiling legislations between 1958 to 1971, only one million hectare has been declared surplus, i.e. 0.7 per cent of the net cropped area. Less than half of this has been redistributed to the weaker sections. This is when 4 per cent of the rural population control 31 per cent of the land area. The apparent decline in percentage of holdings by very big landowners is not due to ceilings. It was more the result of partition of holdings due to inheritance and transfer of land by the big landholders to their other family members, kinsmen, servants, temples and even domesticated animals (Sic !). Therefore in reality, there is no major break in the concentration of land in a few hands. In fact, percentage of holding above 10 hectares have by and large remained constant (approximately 25 per cent control 75 per cent of land) over the last sixty years. Many Zamindars, rich feudal lords, ex-princes have managed to retain thousands of acres of land in their possession (for instance, D. V. Reddy and Challapalli Raja of Andhra Pradesh; Balangir Raja of Orissa; Ganga Naidu, A. S. Chakkarai, N. C. Manradiar and Dharmapuram Mutt trust (72,000 acres) of Tamil Nadu; Darbhanga Raja, Sahu (20,000 acres) and two Mahants of Bodh-

Gaya and Baudouli of Bihar; and even the Birla House in a number of states). Thus the ceiling legislations have mostly been an outright sham. The declared surplus is an eloquent testimony to the utter bankruptcy of the policy.

Meanwhile, the little surplus land acquired by paying huge amounts of compensation was largely found unfit for cultivation and distributed to the landless peasants at higher prices than the compensation paid per plot. This means our landless farmers are supposed to be in a position to buy land from the state, which intends to have a profit in land reforms if not in the land business. Further, the landless allottees sometimes do not have the guarantee of using that land as the big landlords try terrorist measures to prevent them going to the plots; and if they complain, they are often implicated under one or other section of the Indian Penal Code.

Obviously, in a society whose laws are fundamentally rooted on the inviolability of Private Property, the ceiling legislations involving some degree of expropriation of property rights and thereby restructuring property relations have hardly any chance of success.

The other major reform was the tenancy reform aimed at security of tenants, regulation of rent and change from crop share to fixed rent. It's sucess, if it can be called so, only benefited a small section of upper tenants i.e. the tenants-in-chief who already had stable rights, while the conditions of the large masses of unprotected crop-sharers and sub-tenants got worse with large scale evictions, high rent and more difficult conditions of work. Lack of records of tenants in many parts of the country frustrated the legislation. It has remained ineffective as the small tenants seldom insist on their legal rights without endangering their existence. The local landlords not only control political and legal institutions and provide credit and part-time employment but also threaten to evict the potentially troublesome tenants by resuming the land for 'self cultivation'. Both bureaucracy and judiciary generally remain apathetic to the tenants' claims, even when it is made. They themselves are often substantial landowners or have close association with the landed interests. Under such circumstances, granting of occupancy rights to tenants and sharecroppers is well-nigh impossible In other words, without redistribution of rural political power through redistribution of land and politicisation of the real and potential beneficiaries, the tenancy reform would never work.

The brief review of land reform legislation reveals that the underlying objective has been to develop entrepreneurial modernization in agriculture. The princes, zamindars, feudal overlords, absentee landlords, and other big landowners are allowed to retain sizeable land under their possession. The big tenants were given occupancy rights. Hardly any land is redistributed among the small peasants and agricultural labourers. Feudal forms of tenure have been replaced by secured variants with fixed cash rent and cost-share leases. Meanwhile, after the food crisis in 1964-65, the planners strongly felt that without large scale intervention and subsidies from the Government, it was impossible to overcome economic stagnation. Accordingly, side-tracking the issue of land reform, the strategy of promoting the green revolution was introduced to enhance agricultural production. In some pockets, the wealthier landowners received a disproportionate share of governmental assistance through a number of subsidies. After all, control of land and access to technical and other help are closely associated. This further accentuated the problem of inequality in the limited areas affected by the green revolution. Barring a few pockets, most parts of the country continue to have backward pre-capitalist form of agriculture. Once again, disappointment with the pace of agricultural growth and the pressure of popular peasant movements in some parts of India during late 1960s and early 1970s led to a greater commitment to land reform and land redistribution. But the overall approach to the problem has remained basically the same, i.e. primarily intending to serve the Indian industy.

Small wonder, even the official sources, once in a while, acknowledge the failure of land reform measures, specially the ceiling legislations. They agree that there has been a wide gap between the enactment of laws and their implementation. And the formal objectives of land reforms are frustrated because of the lack of political commitment and administrative capability at the lower level. But these, by themselves, are only of superficial and partial significance. Laws are made infructuous and thwarted not simply by the cumbersome administrative procedures nor because of the frantic scurrying and manoeuvring of the political elite but *because of the character of the state, the political strength of the feudal landlords Vs. that of the capitalists, and the state of existence and consciousness of the actual and potential beneficiaries from the land reforms.*

Land reform is essentially a question of redistribution of political power, specially as it sought to redistribute right in land and promote institutional developments. It necessarily invites a shift in the power equations from one class to another. Therefore, it cannot be accomplished without disrupting social structures. When it is inspired and executed not by an organized peasantry but by the state from above, its significance depends upon the objectives and interests pursued by those who hold power. The experience is that all the national political parties, irrespective of their ideologies have indulged in radical talk and introduced legislations in order to divert and temporarily stall the agrarian struggles and to mobilise the votes of the poor for maintaining and acquiring power rather than for generating social and economic development. The entrenched bureaucracy has taken advantage of this ambivalence. It has hardly resisted even deliberate subversion of legislative provisions by the landed interests.

Here the pertinent question is, how could such a phenomenon continue for such a long time ? This shows the failure of the Indian industry to eradicate feudal relations. In fact, several big industrial houses, notwithstanding their support for progressive land legislations, have substantial interest in land. The green revolution has perhaps benefitted international capital more than it has Indian industry. At the same time, the experience of land reform shows that any attempt to alienate the landlords from the power echelon of the country is doomed to be a failure. No political party can act against the landed interests solidly without undermining the very political base. It is only when feudal power and imperialist domination is destroyed that agriculture can be developed and industrialization become possible.

Now the primary issue is how to eliminate the obscurantist forces in agriculture. History teaches that it is only the toilIng people who can overthrow the lingering feudal system. Agrarian reform can be a reality only by organising the rural poor on a nation-wide scale. They must take their lives in their hands, take courage and efficiently meet even the armed attacks of the rich landlords and their articulate allies, and redistribute the land amongst themselves, if necessary by force. Without building and unleashing a comprehensive class conscious organization of the toiling masses in rural areas, no qualitative change in land structure and development is practicable. *Thus, the mass organisation and its militant intervention remains a prerequisite for effective implementation of land reforms.* And as long as the potential beneficiaries of agrarian reform are at a precariously marginal state of existence without any choice of alternatives and remain unorganised and inarticulate the success of land reforms may best be left to election manifestos and close door academic discussions. The state, however, by its very nature, while passing off perverted measures as socialism may prove to be quick in dismantling and repressing any attempt to organise the masses on revolutionary lines to achieve greater equality by means of compulsory take over of land from the big landowners and its redistribution, as, according to some interpretations, it did earlier in Telengana, Naxalbari and Srikakulam. The state, by itself will continue to have a balance between, on the one hand, its defence of private property in land and development of the rich peasantry, and, on the other, its attempts to curtail the peasant movements at whatever cost.

In this context, let us see how Indian Sociology can contribute towards our understanding of and changing of the moribund system. So far, most of the Indian sociologists and social anthropologists have confined to an a-historical, structural-functional framework. They have managed to gloss over the real agrarian issues. The limited attention on the impact of land reforms is carried out within the 'modernization' syndrome; wherein the role of the tillers were taken up as bearer of tradition, passive and dormant. It is hardly necessary to stress that such a framework and perspective is detrimental to both knowledge and practice.

The most significant areas in agrarian reform demanding a knowledge of Sociology appears to be the analysis of the class character of the State and law; the contradictions between the ruling classes and their relative strength, including regional variations; the relative autonomy of the State; comparative study of the impact of the land legislations on the rural power structure between the green revolution areas and the backward areas; social background of the political and administrative elite and representation of class interests in policy formulations and implementations; role of the caste in legalising extra-economic coercion against the lower caste labourers and forwarding agrarian conflicts as caste conflicts; role of peasant movements in land reform legislations; peasant movements and the reaction of the state; and the problems and strategies of organising the masses to achieve greater equality. Obviously, such studies need an overhaul change in the existing orientation of social research, theoretically, methodologically and conceptually.

# 7

# THE UNITED STATES INTERVENTION IN THIRD WORLD RURAL POLICIES

During the 1950s and early 1960s, several U.S. foundations, notably the Ford Foundation, spread the message of community development to Third World governments (Srinivas and Panini, 1973 : 199). Douglas Ensminger of the Ford Foundation played a crucial role in selling the strategy to the Indian government. He enjoyed ready access to the Prime Minister, cabinet ministers. Planning Commission, and top bureaucrats. Recently he recalled : I fed program ideas into India through the same channels. To keep me informed the Planning Commission sent me . . . its working documents . . . with an understanding that ideas and suggestions from me were always welcome. The Planning Commission always expected feedback of my critical observations following a field trip —and this I did. (cited in Rosen, 1985-53).

In fact for over fifteen years, the office of the Ford Foundation in New Delhi was regarded as a participant in the generation of ideas and in developing new rural development program strategies. In 1952, Ensminger procured $2.2 million from the Ford Foundation for village development projects and training centres for rural leaders in India and Pakistan. In a few months, the mammoth community development programme was formally launched with an average annual assistance of $5 million from the

(This paper was presented at a seminar on "Problem and Prospects of Rural Malaysia", held at Consumers' Association of Penang, Malaysia, 22-26 Nov., 1985).

Ford Foundation and a total of about $14 million from the U.S. Department of Agriculture and USAID (Chandrasekhar, 1965; 155).

Likewise in the late 1950s, the Comilla experiment in East Pakistan was carried out by the Ford Foundation with technical help from Michigan University. The Pueblo projects in Mexico, Lilongve land development programme in Malavi, Jezira settlement scheme in Sudan, and the Rural Reconstruction movement in Thailand, are some of the well-known foreign inspired community development experiments. Notwithstanding marginal differences between these projects, the common objectives were to increase agricultural production by stimulating farmers to farm on modern lines and thereby, bring rural society into the matrix of the national and international economy. This comprehensive self-help movement was expected to land the Third World to a 'take-off' stage of development. It was designed to promote a better quality of life for the whole community and to evoke community participation in all developmental activities. In some countries, the *Panchayati-raj* type 'decentralised' administrative infrastructure was created to effectively implement this rural development policy.

The striking postulate of the policy was that planning and execution were to be based on traditions and cultural values of the people and all households involved in a spirit of co-operation in an informal consensus mechanism. Ignoring inherited disparities in the rural social structure was instrumental in widening the already existing divisions among the various agrarian classes. Subsidized inputs, credit, extension services, marketing and other advantages went to the substantial farmers while the poor majority continued to remain outside the organization and functioning of the program (Dube, 1967 : 82-83). The *Panchayati Raj* instead of restructuring rural power, legitimised and consolidated the already existing political inequality (Pathy, 1981).

The crux of the programme was the idea that exogenous forces alone could stimulate the motivation for change in rural society. This facilitated adoption of Western technologies and 'aid'.

Leave alone the political leadership, even the so-called value free scholars, never questioned the political and ideological significance of the programme which originated from a doubtful source. Instead they reacted favourably. However, the scarcity of food and employment led to unrest among the rural poor and forced the international and national planners to reorient the rural policy.

## PRELUDE TO GREEN REVOLUTION

In the 1960s, Community Development Schemes became more and more shallow and were finally dropped altogether. Ensminger of the Ford Foundation had already suggested that the Indian Prime Minister and Planning Commission seek the advice of American experts. Accordingly, the chief econonmist of the U.S. Department of Agriculture, S. Johnson, had headed a team which presented the Food Crisis Report in 1959. The recommendations included higher price for food grains, increased distribution of technical fertilizers, managerial improvement of water supplies, and concentration of development efforts in irrigated areas with the highest potential to raise grain output. The Indian government accepted the Ten-point Intensive Agricultural District Program (IADP) in 1960. The Ford Foundation, contributing $10.5 million. pioneered the IADP in fifteen districts in, 1961; it was subsequently extended to 114 districts by 1965. When the Ministry of Food and Agriculture showed some reluctance. Ensminger threatened that they would withdraw aid unless the Indian government met its commitment (Rosen, 1985 : 77). The Ford Foundation, thus succeeded in rearing its brainchild, the IADP. This developed strategy, overtly concentrated on the rural rich in development regions and supplied them with liberal credit, subsidized inputs, price-incentives, technical advice and market facilities.

Although Ford Foundation was instrumental in implementing this elitist technocratic approach to agricultural development, the American Embassy USAID mission, the MIT Centre, Peace Corps, World Bank and Rockefeller Foundation, to name only the most important influencing agents, forced India to rely more on market incentives to raise farm output. It is worth noting that since 1955, the MIT centre under the directorship of Max Millikan, the Ex-CIA director of economic research, was involved to extensive fieldwork and operational research on Indian planning. It also co-operated with Indian research institutions and provided fellowships to train Indian scholars in the United States. The Centre thus influenced the overall strategy of the Second and Third Five Year Plans of India. The MIT Centre received grants from the Ford Foundation for ten years. Its director has this to say of the role of the Centre : Certainly from the standpoint of our being helpful to the U.S. government, this is the part of our programme which has paid the biggest dividends so far . . . .(we) are now having some real influence in Washington. (Cited in Rosen, 1985 : 113).

Like its financier—the Ford Foundation—the MIT centre pleaded for a change in rural policy. Though the centre was forced to relinquish its surveillance in 1965, when its CIA connections were exposed, it had already manipulated a support base among self-seeking university teachers, politicians, members of the Planning Commission, and the bureaucracy.

Similarly, the Ford Foundation impressed upon the Pakistan government to establish a powerful planning commission under the expert guidance of Harvard University faculty. With the advent of Ayub Khan's regime in Pakistan, the insidious takeover of the Planning Commission by American experts was complete (Waterston, 1963). Klemme of the Ford Foundation in Pakistan brought his office into a key area of policy making. The Harvard Advisory Group (HAG) received support to the tune of $7 million during 1962-70 from the Ford Foundation, USAID, and World Bank. Richard Gilbert of the HAG influenced economic policy in Pakistan during three Five Year Plans. In addition, the Ford Foundation played a crucial role in establishing the Pakistan Institute of Development Economics (PIDE). This Institute received grants of about $3 million during 1959-69, and was backed by a series of American Universities (Rosen, 1985: 66-67). In the early 1960s, all these agencies were responsible for a farm policy concentrating on sustantial farmers in well endowed areas.

The Ford Foundation provided funds to Syracuse University

and the Massachusetts Institute of Technology (MIT) to finance programs for sending Americans overseas for two years to work inside the governments of the Third World in order to 'help' them and prepare worthwhile agricultural development projects. This, U.S. government too spent several million dollars in dozens of countries through similar projects. The USAID had similar overseas project contracts with some 71 U.S. Universities in 1964, involving about $ 165 million (Evans, 1969 : 66, 182). These scholars,besides advising Third World governments, represented them in negotiating loans from the World Bank (e.g. Kenya), and were employed in several regional economic development organizations (e.g. Colombia). With a few exceptions, they argued for a new deal for Third World agriculture that essentially prepared a fertile ground for the implementation of the so-called 'green revolution'.

## GREEN REVOLUTION MIRACLE: SELL OUT TO THE U.S.

The Norman E. Borlaug team's momentous discovery of high yielding varieties (HYVs) of wheat, generously supported by the Rockefeller Foundation, was advertised as the panacea for all food problems in the Third World. Theodore Schultz's, *Transforming Traditional Agriculture* provided the agro-economic justification. The U.S. agencies contributed financial and ideological support to implement the strategy. Basically, the strategy was designed to increase agricultural output in the Third World by creating a narrow stratum of capitalist farmers, termed 'model farmers'. It also aimed at integrating agricultural production with the market economy, both domestic and international. The crucial thrust of the strategy was to enhance the dependence of the Third World on foreign capital, technology, know-how, seeds, pesticides, fertilisers, agricultural machinery etc. It was soon introduced in Pakistan, Nigeria, Colombia, Phillipines, Ethiopia, Bangladesh and India.

At the behest of World Bank and USAID, the Third Five Year Plan (1968-73) of Ethiopia stimulated green revolution and export oriented agricultural production (Sisaye and Stommes,

1980 : 163). The implementation of individual projects remained under the control of the World Bank or USAID.

The HYV package reached India in 1966-67. Wheat production increased from 12 million tonnes in 1967 to 26 million tonnes in 1972. But the early promise was not maintained (Palmer, 1973). During 1975-85, foodgrain production expanded at 2.4 percent per annum. But significantly, the per capita availability of foodgrain fell from 470 gm per day in 1961 to 438 gm in 1984, when India harvested the biggest crop in its history (151.4 million tonnes). There has been a conspicuous decline in per capita production of foodgrains in some parts of India. For example, during 1973-83, it declined from 170 kg to 110 kg in West Bengal, from 63 to 45 kg in Kerala, and from 263 to 187 kg in Rajasthan. Although 26 million tonnes of food grains are stored in government warehouses, only 0.3 million tonnes have been given for Food for Work programmes and more than half of the Indian population, lacking purchasing power, go to bed on half-empty stomachs.

That the green revolution strategy, being capital and technology intensive, aggravates inequality and increases unemployment has now been definitively established. The process of depeasantization has been accelerated and rural poverty and unemployment increased. Hence, notwithstanding the technological changes in certain regions, the old relations of production, bondage and servitude continued although in different forms (Saini, 1976 : 1804-6). The direct cultivators have been forced to substitute traditional techniques through indebtedness (Rayer, 1980). The green revolution displaced legumes in the traditional diet of the poor and intensified their protein-calorie malnutrition. This rural improverishment and nutritional deterioration is common throughout the Third World.

Initially, we were told that the HYV seed-fertiliser-irrigation-technology was scale neutral and that small farmers would benefit as much as large farmers. But it is an established fact that despite high rates of growth, the incidence of rural poverty has increased. World Bank itself estimated in 1980 that over 750 million people or about 20 per cent of world's population lived in absolute poverty (World Bank, 1981).

The Third World rural crisis is not merely a crisis of production, but also one of distribution (Jacoby, 1975). The arguments that faster and faster increase in production would alleviate poverty, thus, cannot be supported.

Who reaped the maximum benefit from the package ? Obviously the multinational corporations manufacturing fertiliser, pesticide and tractors. It is estimated that about 60 per cent of the cost of production of wheat in the new strategy finds its way into imports (Sau, 1972 : 1575). In 1977, Cargill and Continental Grain cornered the market on HYV wheat multiplied in Mexico for global distribution (Morgan, 1979). The giant U.S. farm-machine company, Massey-Ferguson, has been busy selling tractors to green revolution farmers. Several U.S. companies like International Harvester and Caterpillar, with their obsolete technology, have invested in the productions of farm equipment in the Third World Multinational Corporation and have often joined 'aid' giving agencies to block technological developments in fertiliser, pesticides (Mehta, 1983). The World Bank played an important role in undermining local interests (Menon, 1980). There is growing evidence that MNCs have been dumping hazardous pesticides which are banned or severely restricted in their home countries (Rahman, 1983 : 80). The highly toxic pesticides causing cancer in human beings are aldrin, chlordane, endrin, lindane etc. They are freely used in the Third World. The FAO has estimated that on an average 10,000 persons die every year due to pesticide poisoning. There seems to be little awakening in the Third World about pesticides poisoning and acute toxicity resulting in death in many cases. There is an alternative to the massive use of chemical fertilisers, pesticides and farm machinery, which involves little capital while absorbing a great deal of human labour (FAO, 1976). But it remains unutilised in the interests of the MNCs.

With the green revolution sweeping across the world, more and more invaluable and irreplaceable genes have disappeared. Today, the USA holds 22 percent of the world germ-plasm collection followed by USSR (7 per cent). India and Malayasia (6 per cent each). Germ-plasm is the genetic character added to new varieties of crops. The substantial majority of this germ-plasm lies in the Third World, but it has been bred in the North, specially the United States, which markets its new varieties at great profit around the world. The pace of genetic erosion is so profound that before the end of this century, most of the crop germ-plasm will be gone and the world will be left with a handful of amorphous collections of highly vulnerable HYVs (Mooney,1983). A few of the large MNCs led by Royal Dutch/Shell, Ciba-Geigy and Sandoz have acquired hundreds of seed companies and have aggressively moved into the Third World with their plant-breeding biotechnology, pesticides and herbicides.

## EXPORT-ORIENTED AGRICULTURE : A TREAT FOR MULTINATIONAL AGRIBUSINESS

The gamut of U.S. inspired and promoted rural policies in the Third World, remains incomplete without a consideration of export-oriented agricultural strategy and the shedding of crocodile tears for the rural underprivileged. In recent years, there has been a phenomenal increase in direct and indirect agribusiness. Within a short time, Thailand, for instance, became the biggest exporter of bananas largely due to the U.S. Company, Castle and Cook. The U.S. government recognised:

> Some of the best investments and sales opportunities for American companies in Thailand continue to be in the agribusiness sector. With the government's development plans. . .sales prospects look particularly good for exporters of agricultural and food processing machinery and equipment as well as a wide variety of products and services needed for planned development of the rural economy (USA, 1977).

Likewise, the major exportable agricultural commodity is groundnuts in Senegal and Niger; coffee in Colombia, Haiti, El-Salvador, Guatemala, Brazil and Ethiopia; tea in Sri Lanka; cocoa in Ghana; sugar in Hawaii, Philippines, Indonesia and Thailand; and so on. The MNCs dominate the trade. For example, just three MNCs control 75 per cent of the banana trade, six account for 70 per cent of the cocoa trade, and another six control 85 to 90 per cent of trade in leaf tobacco (TWN, 1985 : 21). The area under export-crop cultivation is expanding at the cost of food crops. For instance, in the Philippines, land area devoted to export crops has increased from about 35 per cent of food crop land in 1963 to almost 45 per cent by 1976. In Malayasia, the percentage of total crop devoted to rubber, oil palm and coconuts has risen from 74 per cent in 1960 to 86 per cent in 1975 (Young *et ul.*, 1980:218-219). At the inspiration of IMF-World Bank, the Sri Lanka government announced in 1983 that about 14000 hectares of land under the accelerated Mahaweli programme would be available for technology oriented 'non-peasants' of the 'higher income group' for crops like cotton, sugarcane, soyabean and vegetables (Shanmugaratnam, 1984). In Chiapas state of Mexico, most of the suitable land has been turned over to coffee production. In Central America and the Caribbean, more than half the agricultural land has been put under cultivation for export (Collins and Lappe, 1977).

Mexico supplies U.S. with more than half its vegetables while infant deaths associated with malnutrition are common. Half of central America's agricultural produce is exported whereas a third of her people consume loss than half of the required protein intake. Africa's which has a higher incidence of protein-calorie malnutrition, is ironically a net exporter of barley, beans, peanuts, fresh vegetables and cattle (Lappe and Collins, 1977:15).

U.S. based MNCs have been purchasing land in several Third World countries. For instance, between 1964-70, they bought nearly 32 to 35 million hectares of agricultural land in Brazil alone (Feder, 1977 : 563). Of course, U.S. citizens and corporations enjoy 'parity rights' with local citizens in over a dozen countries like the Philippines in matters of exploiting and utilising agricultural land, forest resources and minerals, and in running public utilities. Crops being subject to international price fluctuations, the fortunes of even the substantial cash-crop producing peasants remain uncertain. On the other hand, the MNCs make huge profits from cheap labour and benefit from funds and services of government agricultural programs.

U. S. agencies including IBRD and IMF have been encouraging export-oriented agricultural growth in the Third World Countries. For example, Togo, receiving $ 10 million from the World Bank in 1974, found that the total amount was earmarked solely for the development of cash crops like coffee and cocoa (Dumont and Cohen, 1980 : 35). Similarly, since 1977, the World Bank strategy for agricultural development in Sri Lanka emphasised and provided subsidies for replanting and fertilising export crop plantations and agro-industries and sought incentives like tax holidays for non-traditional exports and processing of sugar, milk-products, livestock production and fisheries (Shanmugaratnam, 1984). About half of the World Bank's allotment to agricultural projects in Brazil, Paraguay and Chile is reserved for cattle raising for export. The Latin American Agribusiness Corporation, which was founded by the Bank of America and received $ 17 million from USAID, assists in this drainage of food stuffs from Latin America.

## 'CONCERN' FOR RURAL POOR

In the mid 1970s, several of these agencies responsible for escalating rural unemployment, hunger, poverty and illiteracy, suddenly seemed to have realised that something ought to be done for the rural poor—the small peasants, tenants, and landless. World Bank led the way. It observed that "rural development is a strategy to improve the economic and social life of the rural poor," "to reduce poverty, increase production and raise productivity", "to modernise and monetize rural society". However, it did not alter its emphasis on "lending to larger scale farmers when it is necessary to raise their production in order to increase food supply and/or contribute to exports" (IBRD, 1975 : 3, 12). The reformulation from 'trickle down' theory was more to legitimize foreign aid in the eves of the public than a strategy for the rural poor. Billions of dollars continued to be channeled towards the landed elite, either directly by supporting the commodities they produce (e.g. live-stock) or indirectly by financing projects which benefitted most, such as irrigation schemes and roads. Loan projects serve to enhance the sales and profits of multinational agribusiness (Feder, 1977; Falcon, 1970). Finally, the concern for the absolute poor is also aimed at benefitting the privileged, McNamara said, "a continual increase in inequality gives rise to a growing danger for the political stability... In the long run this development will be an advantage for the privileged, as also for the poor" (cited in Bennoholdt, Thomson, 1980 : 17).

Programmes like Food for Work and Rural Works Programme (RWP) were implemented in several countries, which got support not only from the World Bank but also USAID, as in Bangladesh. World Bank cautioned that these programmes should not be undertaken in a manner which would antagonize the richer enterprising section of the areas. Small wonder, that these schemes have strengthened the power of the dominant classes. In India, there are special programmes for smaller farmers (SFDA), marginal farmers and agricultural labourers (MFAL), besides of course, FFW, National Minimum Needs Programme (NMEP), National Rural Employment Programme, (NREP) and Integrated Rural Development Programme (IRDP). The actual expenditure is so paltry that it requires no scepticism to conclude that these schemes concentrate on a group much small than the national target group; nonetheless, it did temporarily counteract the rising disillusionment among the masses. Meanwhile, households below the poverty line have increased from 38 per cent in 1961 to 48 per cent in 1978. And in 1980, the official estimate was 249 million below the poverty line i. e. more than half the total population.

With all the concern for the poor, 450,000,000 people in the world suffer from hunger and malnutrition, 500,000,000 people are unemployed, 870,000,000 cannot read and write, and 2,000,000,000 people do not have safe water to drink (Sivard, 1981).

The rural policies discussed above bring out clearly the role played by the U.S. and its various agencies. The following section deals with the mechanisms through which they persuade and pressurise 'independent' Third World countries to accept such strategies.

## POLITICS OF AID

The United States' foreign aid is extended to obtain immediate economic gains for U.S. businessmen, and enforce 'open door' policies facilitating freedom of access to raw materials, trade and investment opportunities. This ensures increasing economic, political and military dependence on the U.S. by the receivers of the aid (Magdoff, 1969). As President Kennedy put it :

Foreign aid is a method by which the U.S. maintains a position of influence and control around the world, and sustains a good many countries which would definitely collapse or pass into the communist bloc (Cited in Magdoff, 1969:117).

The ex-president of World Bank, Eugene R. Black asserts :
Our foreign aid programs constitute a distant benefit to American business. . . provides a sustantial and immediate market for U.S. goods and services . . . stimulates development of new overseas markets for U.S. companies . . .Orients national economies toward a free enterprise system in which U.S. firms can prosper (Black, 1965 : 23).

The U.S. works out what it wants its debtors to do. In India, as elsewhere, they have been putting pressure on the Indian government to widen the sphere of operation for private capital in general and for foreign private capital in particular. When India faced exchange problems in 1956-57, the government approached the World Bank for help. Its chairman, Eugene Black, replied to the Indian minister of finance in September. . . 1956.

I should like to emphasise once again that India's interest lies in giving private enterprise, both Indian and foreign, every encouragement to make its maximum contribution to the development of the economy . . . I have the distinct impression that the potentialities of private enterprise are commonly underestimated in India and that its operations are subject to unnecessary restrictions there... We feel that we have to consider the pace and scale of our further loan operations in India from time to time in the light of economic conditions and prospects and taking into consideration the economic policies pursued by your government" (cited in Das Gupta, 1970:276).

Willy-nilly, the Indian government accepted the dictation and assured the Bank that it was not at all hostile to private enterprise, domestic or foreign. A temporary salvation package for the Indian plan followed. Foreign private investment increased from $ 1007 million to $ 2104 million between December 1956 and March 1965. Meanwhile, in 1964, a World Bank team headed by Bernard Bell called for severe devaluation of the Indian currency, abolition of many remaining trade controls and an emphasis on high technology agriculture. Abruptly the U.S. food aid was suspended : India was warned by the U.S. against accepting Russian aid (Paver, 1975 : 174). This was the time when India faced a major food shortage and was involved in the Indo-Pakistan war. India was forced in 1966 to a massive devaluation (37.5 per cent) of its currency. The same year, the World Bank and USAID exerted specific pressure for favourable conditions for foreign investment in India's fertilizer industry, import liberalization and elimination of most domestic controls as well. The USAID provided funds for importing fertiliser, but when some U.S. companies refused to accept the Indian government's plea to have its own pricing and distribution system, the USAID, put food shipments from the U.S. on a month to month basis until India let Standard Oil of Indian market fertiliser at its own prices. At the same time, part of the price paid for the 20 million tonnes of wheat shipped from the U.S. as food aid during the two critical years, was the acquisition of a controlling interest in supposedly Indian fertiliser companies by American companies (Dumont and Cohen, 1974 : 173).

Food aid to the Third World under PL 480 was accounted for at the prices on the protected home market in the United States, which was much higher than the internationl market price. Shipping was also reserved for American protected high cost shipping and charged to the aid receiving country.

The disposal of bulging food surpluses at that time was very much in the U.S. interest. Indeed anything from 70 to 90 per cent of 'aid' funds were earmarked for imports from the imperialist powers at high prices. Aid became an instrument of direct political influence and dictation. In 1966, the U.S. openly threatened discontinuation of aid to Guinea in reply to its government's decision to expel the notorious U.S. Peace Corps members from the country. Likewise in 1963, the U.S. government threatened that no aid would be given to Latin American governments if they failed to break economic contacts with Cuba within sixty days. Similar denial or termination of aid has been frequently used to call to order or punish recalcitrant Third World governments.

And yet the Third World's dependence on foreign aid from the U.S. and its agents seems to be insatiable. In 1984, the foreign debt of the Third World exceeded the figure of $ 810 billion. In 1981, the annual interest payments on foreign debts was $ 51 billion. About one-fourth of the export earnings of non-oil developing countries have to be set aside for debt servicing alone. In several countries like Brazil, Mexico, Argentina, Venezuela, Zambia, Bolivia and Peru, the annual debt service payment accounts for more than their total earnings from exports. In 1982, the gross foreign borrowing of Third World countries amounted to $ 140 billion of which debt servicing constituted 77 per cent of the total loan.

Countries that apply to the IMF for short-term loans to stabilize their currencies are usually in desperate or close to desperate straits. The IMF sets up conditions before handing out the money, that fulfill the goals of the U.S. administration by enforcing the rules of the game. It insists on elimination of controls over imports and exports, free exchange rates, devaluation of the local currency and strong fiscal controls within the country by institution of wage and price controls and balanced budget (Payer, 1975).

When Latin economies were found incapable of meeting their foreign debt obligations, the U.S. and IMF compelled the debtors to give priority to increasing their foreign exchange receipts. Twelve Latin American countries signed the conditionality agreement with the IMF in 1982-83 alone. The IMF recipe of reduced public spending, import cuts, export stimuli, salary freezes etc., to raise extra surplus for debt servicing resulted in sharp cuts in social expenditures and the strict 'austerity' programmes had serious political ramifications in Brazil, Morocco, Tunisia, Egypt, Philippines, Sudan and other places. In the Philippines, foreign debt shot up to a whopping $ 26 billion from $ 2 billion in 1972. The Peso is regularly devalued even as inflation and unemployment reach new heights. In Peru, with an external debt of $ 14 billion, inflation rose from 73 per cent in 1981 to 106 per cent in 1984 and in 1983, unemployment and underemployment reached a staggering 63 per cent of the economically active population. In Bolivia, inflation rose from 25 per cent in 1981 to 328 per cent in 1983 to 2177 per cent in 1984 and is now over 3000 per cent. Interest obligations on foreign debt amount to about $ 400 million a year (Herman and Petras, 1985 : 1151). In Uganda, a U.S. dollar was equal to some 60 Ugandian shillings in 1980; it is now 650 shillings. IMF loans have led to immiseration and pauperisation of the working people. At the same time, the debt crisis is enhanced. Consequently, Peru recently refused to negotiate with the IMF and restricted foreign debt payments to ten per cent of export earnings.

The consequences of the 'structural adjustment' programmes forced upon Third World countries by the IMF as *quid pro quo* for the rescheduling of their debt to multinational commercial banks has been plainly disastrous for these countries. A sharp decline in lending of American commercial banks, as also resultant socio-political unrest in client states like Chile, Mexico, Philippines etc., has prompted a shift in U.S. policy to 'growth oriented approach' to the Third World problem of debt, as was evident from the annual meet of IMF and IBRD at Seoul in September, 1985.

On an average $ 4.5 came as income into the U.S. for each dollar invested in the Third World. In absolute terms, the total income received on U.S. foreign investments rose from less than $ 2 billion in 1950 to $ 11 billion in 1970 and $ 76 billion in 1980. And additionally, U.S. and U.S. agents collected sensitive and vital information on the Third World. For instance, World Bank's Policy of 'global tender' not only ensures penetration of MNCs into the Third World, but also its experts investigate the general political economy of the country at the cost of project funds. In several countries it maintains permanent missions to advise on various economic and political issues.

Why do Third World governments and people not see the merit of self-reliance ? In most cases, they cannot escape the trap without a radical restructuring of their internal political system and its place in international socio-political relations. Thus, a large number of societies depend more or less solely on international capital for development. Take for instance Bangladesh where foreign aid accounts for virtually the whole of the development budget. It therefore accepts all terms and conditions, dictates and interferences. The influence of World Bank, IMF, and the U.S. embassy has become a pervasive phenomenon in the country's economic, social, cultural and political life. Though total aid has been increasing and stood at about $ 17 billion in 1984, about 85 per cent of the population is now below the poverty line and 60 per cent is critically poor. Forty per cent of the available labour time is unemployed (Ahmad, 1985 : 30-37). To some extent, the same was the case with Sri Lanka during 1965-69 and again since 1977, when the IMF-World Bank-U.S. shaped the "liberalisation Policy." In 1980-84, more than 60 per cent of the budgetary provision for rural development depended on foreign assistance. Besides, the funding of the Integrated Rural Development Projects in nine districts came from U.S. agencies (Shanmugaratnam, 1985; Lakshman, 1985).

## INDOCTRINATION AND THE 'CAPTIVE MIND'

There is a social basis for the articulation of foreign interests Training and institution building are more essential here than outright distribution of patronage. U.S. agencies have given considerable emphasis to training, research, extension services and influencing researchers and academics in the Third World.

In India, as in almost all Third World Countries, various U.S. agencies have acquired control over the entire field of agricultural education, reaearch and extension. This control has been systematically utilised for pushing the green revolution and export-oriented cropping. Consequently, there is little work on dry farming practices, high protein crops, incorporation of local germplasm in plantbreeding, appropriate soil and water conservation policies, and suitable crop rotation patterns to reduce dependence on chemical fertiliser and pesticides (Abrol, 1983).

Indo-U.S. co-operation in agricultural research dates back to the efforts of the U.S. government to help India increase food production. In 1953, F.W. Parker of the Technical Co-operative Mission arranged a number of studies determining the fertility status of soils. This laid the basis for the establishment of a chain of soil testing laboratories aided by USAID which subsequently paved the way for the introduction of chemical fertilisers in India. In 1955, Rockefeller Foundation and five U.S. land grant universities assisted Indian agricultural universities and research institutions and suggested a curricula appropriate to reorienting scholars to meet the challenge of introducing HYVs of maize, sorghum and millets. The U.S. gave $ 35 million for laboratory equipment and libraries. Every year, 35 fellowships were instituted for training Indian students at U.S. institutions. Rockefellers provided $ 21.3 million upto 1973 and arranged for several visiting professors to visit India. It also provided travel grants for Indian government officials and university administrators to go to the U.S. In 1982, Ralph W. Cummings, the Director of Rockefeller Foundation's Indian agricultural research programme laid down guidelines for the establishment and development of agricultural universities. These guidelines focussed on higher agricultural productivity through diffusion of fertiliser responsive varieties. The narrow genetic base of HYVs, disease and pest suspectibility of some of the parent varieties and the existence of vast monoculture soon exposed the crops to attacks by pests and diseases. As noted earlier, in the mid-1960s, USAID provided large loans to import much needed fertilisers. The U.S. and World Bank put pressure on the Indian government to encourage MNCs investment in local fertiliser production. Such a strategy could not have been pursued smoothly without the support of Indian agricultural scientists trained in the service of American interests (Abrol, 1983).

From 1952-72, the Ford Foundation spent $ 16 million providing generous grants to persons, institutions and government on a wide variety of nation building activities. It established and/or funded the Institute of Economic Growth, Gokhale Institute of Politics and Economics, National Council of Applied Economic Research, Indian Statistical Institute and Institutes of Management at Calcutta and Ahmedabad. The Foundation trained about 50,000 extension workers. The National Institute of Community Development was established with the help of USAID and Michigan State University. The whole pattern of education and research was thus modelled on the philosophy and value system of the donor country. U.S. experts provided advice on how to organise and develop science and technology, decided the priorities of research, recommended developmental models. Performance of major research and educational institutes like UGC, CSIR, ICAR, etc. is reviewed by experts from the U.S. and Western Europe. This delinking of science and technology from the concrete socio-political contexts has proved to be stultifying.

USEFI claims to have sent 2380 Indians to the USA and 1265 American scholars to India between 1952 and 1972. An estimated 5000 Indian were sent to the U.S. for further training by 1965. The exchange programmes, study and research grants are used to glorify the American way of life (Krishna Kumar, 1980). About 7600 U.S. peace corps volunteers are active in 61 Third World countries (Cohn and Wood, 1980). Their major objective is to influence the development choices and prevent any going over to the 'communist camp' (Shriver, 1964 : 50,8). In the Philippines, under the Economic and Technical Cooperation Agreement, 1951, U.S. advisers influenced policies and conducted imperialist propaganda in every strategic branch. Some are on the payroll of the C.I.A. PL. 480 proceeds finance propaganda campaigns and exchange programmes in the receiving country. Similarly, as many as 80 per cent of the social scientists in Ethiopia are trained in North America and approximately 30 per cent of the expatriate academic staff in the University comes from North America. (Jimadu, 1985 : 50-51). Tanzania despite the Arusha declaration, has strong academic relations with the U.S. (Ake, 1979).

Scholars are trained to believe that the backwardness of the Third World is due to cultural reasons, and development is possible only through the continued diffusion of capital, technology, and ideology from Western societies. This perspective of development by totally ignoring class and national exploitation, tacitly eulogises neo-colonial domination and certifies external incentives as the *sine qua non* of development. The model provided perfect justification for pillage (Pathy, 1982 ; Tullis, 1973 ; Frank, 1971). Third World scientists were thus indoctrinated.

American trained professionals, bureaucratic and political dollar addicts and compradores, articulated the interests of the imperialist masters for pecuniary gains. It may be recalled that when Sihanouk rejected U.S. aid in 1963, there was strong opposition from this section which led to the overthrow of the legitimate government and the installation of a puppet regime. In India, many erstwhile employees of the World Bank hold important positions in the Reserve Bank, Prime-Minister's secretariat, economic ministries, and Planning Commission (Bhambhri, 1985). Several bureaucrats are linked with MNCs. Using the techniques of lucrative jobs and other incidental benefits as a *quid pro quo*, imperialism has penetrated the decision making structures of Third World governments and bureaucracies (Bhambhri, 1970). When the conditions of the recent IMF loan were criticised, a powerful lobby of Indian academics, politicians and bureaucrats openly came out in support of IMF and World Bank. One of the top Indian economists, speaking against the criticism said, the fact that the IMF "an expert storehouse of financial and monetary information concerning most countries of the world," has sanctioned the loan, should itself be "a matter of great jubilation to proponents of the cause of the Third World. . . . That such an organisation should have found India so highly credit worthy is a matter to be deeply pondered over" (Sic.), (Brahmananda, 1982 : 3, 1).

Today some 50,000 U.S. servicemen are stationed all around the world, in some 1500 military installations in 32 countries. In the Philippines, it has as many as 20 military bases, containing nuclear, chemical and bacteriological weapons, that can be used as a launching pad for aggression in Asia and middle-east. The U.S. has openly used biochemical and geophysical weapons against independent, socialist countries. It has perfected a large number of plant-destroying agents, including genetically mutated breeds of pests and rodents.

Without fear of exaggeration, it can be stressed that the expansion of MNCs into the Third World is made possible with the massive and unremitting application of the power of the U.S. and its agencies like World Bank and IMF. This application of power takes place directly as in the Dominican Republic, Vietnam and a long string of CIA-organised coups in Iran, Guatemala, Bangladesh etc. It is done indirectly through funding and arming client dictatorial regimes and sub-imperialist gendarmes to repress their own people. Naked political intervention and subversion including engineered political murders, are too well known to need any recounting here. Inconvenient regimes have been subverted, and uncooperative rulers removed or assassinated to be replaced by more pliable ones. In the Third World, 54 countries are under military rule. Since 1960, there have been at least 76 military coups which, in most cases, ousted liberal and legitimate governments. In this scenario, the contribution of the U.S. government and its agencies is enormous.

The U.S. and the C.I.A. fund reactionary groups and individuals in the Third World when they consider them friendly to U.S. imperialism. They propped up pro-west regimes in Africa, (Zaire, Ivory Coast, Kenya, Sudan, Nigeria and Morocco), which welcomed foreign capital to modernize their countries. But where this was not possible, the U.S. stirred up communal, linguistic, regional movements to destabilise governments. The CIA recruits informants from the government, army, intelligence, education, culture, industry and business. In India, the widely known Himalayan border studies project and more recently project Brahamaputra, sponsored by the CIA, were designed to study ethnic tensions and encourage separatist elements in the country. The CIA maneouvered the rise of Mobutu Seko to power during 1966 while the Congo (Zaire) was in turmoil. (Lemarchand, 1975). It struck at the Sandinista National Liberation Front in Nicaragua, destabilized the Manley government in Jamaica, smuggled mercenary groups into Grenada, and carried out an armed invasion in 1983.

Latin American countries have been saddled with a string of military dictatorship—Brazil, Argentina, Chile, Uruguay, Grenada, Honduras etc.—propped up by U.S. imperialism and sustained by its economic and military aid. Every attempt at reforming the economy, at curbing the power of the oligarchs and multinationals, at democratic reform have been met with stiff resistance, ranging from coups, as in Guatemala and Chile, to direct armed intervention as in the Bay of Pigs crisis. In El Salvador, since late 1979, several thousands have died and many hundred thousands have been driven into exile. There is deliberate and extensive use of fascist terror, repression, mutilation and dismemberment. The Honduras, Grenada and Guatemala dictatorial regimes are utilised against the revolutionary upsurge in Nicaragua, El Salvador and other countries.

To undercut the popular support for the revolutionary forces, the U.S. tried land reforms in El Salvador. But this mimicry of reform failed (Ram, 1983). It was not an unique experiment. To forestall a perceived communist threat, the U.S. inspired such showy land reforms in Taiwan; in Vietnam, the exigencies of counter-insurgency demanded land reform to placate the peasantry. The IMF team advised the military rulers on such reorganization of their economy in Indonesia, Brazil, Argentina etc., soon after elected governments or popular rulers were overthrown.

Yet, the fact that the U. S. has to rely more and more on the use of naked force, on multilateral aid-giving agencies rather than direct interference, demonstrates its weakness in the strategy of cooperation and indoctrination. Everywhere its social basis is eroding, but the weakening trend may make it more brutal.

Rural development in the Third World rests on dismantling the citadels of obscurantist and reactionary national and neo-colonial vested interests. Self-reliance, appropriate technology, new international economic order, basic human needs, approach etc., can have meaning only when there is a fundamental structural transformation of naticnal and international society by the people themselves. Meanwhile, the need is to demystify the operation of the system and contribute to the rise of consciousness of the toiling people.

## *REFERENCES*

Abrol, Dinesh. 1983. "American Involvement in Indian Agricultural Research". *Social Scientist*, XI (10) : 8-26.

Ahmad, Q. K. 1985. "Aid Influence and Development in Bangladesh", *Social Scientists*, XIII (2) : 30-37.

Ake, Claude, 1979. *Social Science as Imperialism : The Theory of Political Development*, Ibadan : Ibadan University Press.

Bennholdt-Thompsen, Veronika. 1980. "Investment on the Poor : Analysis of World Bank Policy", *Social Scientist*, VIII (7) : 3-21.

Bhambhari, C.P. 1970. *Bureaucracy and Politics in India*. Delhi : Vikas.

——— 1985. "Imperialism in India", *Social Scientist*, XIII (2):38-45.

Black, E. R. 1965. "The Domestics Dividends of Foreign Aid", *Columbia Journal of World Business*, Vol. I, Fall.

Brahmanand, P. R. 1982. *The IMF Loan and India's Economic Future*, Bombay : Himalayan Publishing.

Chandrasekhar, S. 1965. *American Aid and India's Economic Development*, New York : Praeger.

Cohn, Steven and Wood, Robert. 1980. "Basic Human Needs Programming : Analysis of Peace Corps Data", *Development and Change*, *XI* (2) : 313-32.

Collins, Joseph and Lappe, F.M. 1970. "Multinational Agribusiness and Global Supermarket", *Social Scientist*, VI (3) : 3-12.

Das Gupta. Ranjit. 1970. *Problems of Economic Transition : Indian Case Study*. Calcutta : National Publishers.

Dhanagare, D.N. 1984. "Agrarian Reforms and Rural Development in India", *Research in Social Movements, Conflicts and Change*, VII : 177-201.

Dhar, Biswajit. 1984. "Factors Influencing Technology Selection", *Economic and Political Weekly*, Annual No. pp. 1485-95.

Dube, S.C. 1967. *India's Changing Villages*, Bombay : Allied.

Dumont, Rene and Cohen, Nicholas, 1980. *The Growth of Hunger, a New Politics of Agriculture*, London : Marion Boyars Publishers Ltd.

Evans, L.H. *et. al.* 1969. *The Decade of Development : Problems and Issues*, Calcutta : Oxford & IBH.

Falcon, W.P. 1970. "The Green Revolution : Generations of Problems", *American Journal of Agricultural Economics*, Vol. 52 : 698-710.

F.A.O. 1976. *Development of a Programme Promoting the Use of Organic Materials as Fertilizers*, Rome : Food and Agricultural Organization.

Feder, Ernest. 1977. "Capitalism's Last Ditch Effort to Save Underdeveloped Agricultures, International Agribusiness, the World Bank and the Rural Poor", *Journal of Contemporary Asia*, VII(1).

—— 1981. "Monopoly Capital and Agricultural Employment in the Third World", *Journal of Contemporary Asia*, XI:135-168.

Frank, A.G. 1971. *The Sociology of Development and the Underdevelopment of Sociology*, London : Pluto Press.

Herman, E.S. and Petras, James. 1985. "Resurgent Democracy in Latin America : Rhetoric and Reality", *Economic and Political Weekly*, XX (27) : 1147-52.

International Bank for Reconstruction and Development (IBRD) 1975. *Rural Development* (Sector Policy Paper), Washington.

Jacoby, E. 1975. "Transnational Corporation and Third World Agriculture", *Development and Change*, IX (1) : 41-70.

Jinadu, L.A. 1985. *The Social Sciences and Development in Africa, Stockholm : SAREC.*

*Krishna Kumar* (ed.) 1980. *Transnational Enterprises : Their Impact on Third World Societies and Cultures*, Boulder, Col. : West View.

Lakshman, W.D. 1985. "The IMF—World Bank Intervention in Sri Lanka Economic Policy : Historical Trends and Patterns", *Social Scientists* XIII (2) : 3-29.

Lappe, F.M. and Collins, Joseph. 1977. *Food First*, Boston : Houghton Miffin.

Lemarchand, R. 1975. "The C.I.A. in Africa", *The Journal of Modern African Studies*, XIV (3) : 401-426.

Magdoff, Harry, 1968. *The Age of Imperialism : The Economics of U.S. Foreign Policy*, New York : Monthly Review Press.

Mehta, Balraj. 1983. "Fertilisers : End of Self Reliance", *Business India*, March 28.

Menon, Usha. 1980. "World Bank and Transfer of Technology —Case of Indian Fertiliser Industry, *Economic and Political Weekly*, August 23, pp. 1437-43.

Mooney, Pat Roy. 1983. "The Law of the Seed : Another Development and Plant Genetic Resources", *Development Dialogue*, Nos. 1-2.

Morgan, Dan. 1979. *Merchants of Grain*, New York : Viking Press.

Navarro, Vicente. 1981. "Genocide in El Salvador", *Monthly Review*, 32 (11).

Palmer, Ingrid. 1973 *How Revolutionary is the Green Revolution ?* London : Voluntary Committee on Overseas Aid and Development.

Pathy, Jagannath, 1981. "Panchayati Raj and Decentralisation of Political Power", *Social Scientist*, No. 93, pp. 36-41.

——, 1982. "Social Anthropology in India", *Association of Third World Anthropologists Bulletin*, III (1-2) : 39-48.

Payer, Cheryl. 1975. *The Debt Trap : The IMF and the Third World, New York, Monthly Review Press.*

——, 1980, "*The World Bank and Small Farmer*" *Monthly Review*, 32 (2).

Rahman, A. 1983. *Intellectual Colonisation : Science and Technology in West-East Relations*, New Delhi : Vikas.

Ram, Susan. 1983. "El Salvador : Perspectives an a Revolutionary Civil War", *Social Scientist*, XI (8) : 3-38.

Rosen, George. 1985. *Western Economists and Eastern Societies*, Delhi : Oxford University Press.

Saini, G.R. 1976. "Green Revolution and Disparities in Farm Incomes", *Economic and Political Weekly* XI (46).

Sau, Ranjit. 1972. "The New Economics", *Economic and Political Weekly*, VII (31-33).

Shanmugaratnam, N. 1984. "Sri Lanka's 'New' Economic Policy and Agriculture", *Social Scientist*, XII (3) : 3-35.

Shriver, Sargent. 1964. *Point of Lance*, New York : Harper and Row.

Sisaye, Seleshi and Stommes, Eileen. 1980. "Agricultural Development in Ethiopia", *The Journal of Development Studies*, XVI (2) : 156-185.

Sivard, R.L. 1981. *World Militaiy and Social Expenditures*, World Priorities.

Srinivas, M.N. and Panini, M.N. 1973. "Development of Sociology and Social Anthropology in India", *Sociological Bulletin*, XII (2).

Third World Network. 1985. *Third World Development of Crisis* ?, Penang : TWN and CAP.

Tullis, F.L.A. 1973. *Politics and Social Change in Third Countries*, New York : John Wiley.

U.S.A. 1977. *Foreign Economic Trends and Their Implications for the United States : Thailand*, U.S. Department of Commerce.

Waterston, Albert. 1963. *Planning in Pakistan*, Baltimore : Johns Hopkins Press.

World Bank. 1981. *World Development Report* : 1981, Washington D.C.

Young, Kevin, *et. al.* 1980. *Malaysia : Growth and Equity in a Multiracial Society*, Baltimore : John Hopkins University Press.

# 8

# POPULATION AND DEVELOPMENT

*In the past 20 years or so, rapid growth of population in the third world countries has become a matter of increasing concern for social scientists at home and abroad. Most, if not all, of them consider the present trend in population increase to be a dreadful menace to the future development of the third world. They argue that the rapidly rising population eats up the few fruits of development, and consequently minimises the saving and investment potential of the already 'overpopulated' third world.*

*The aim of this paper,is to consider the relevance of some of the major propositions concerning the relationship between population and development in the third world. Towards this end, the author outlines in brief the main demographic theories and points out some of the crucial flaws in the basic premise of the neo-Malthusian theory.*

IN THE past 20 years or so, rapid growth of population in the third world countries has become a matter of increasing concern for social scientists—at home and abroad. Most, if not all, of them have considered the present unprecedented trend in population increase to be a dreadful menace to the future development of the third world. They argue that the rapidly rising population eats up the little available fruits of development, and consequently minimises the saving and investment potential of the already 'overpopulated' third world; that, in due course, this may lead to stagnancy or even degeneration of the economy and of society.

Apparently, this neo-Malthusian scare has forced more than 30 governments of the third world to take firm steps to reduce the birth rates in their respective countries. Significantly, far more than the concerned nations, the American government and its multinational foundations have since the beginning of the 1950s shown a keen and cosistent interest in the programme; and they have been spending millions of dollars, accounting for more than half the total expenditure used for the birth control programmes in the third world. Indeed, for the same purpose, 1974 was designated by the United Nations the 'World Population Year'. Obviously, this is grand testimony to the intensity of the population problem.

Even so, we are nowhere near a clearly defined theoretical perspective for understanding the impact of population on development. The nineteenth century controversies, centring around Malthus and Marx, are still the starting points of thinking on population and development. The Malthusian view, that the overpopulation is the main cause for the poverty of the masses and underdevelopment of the societies, is more or less uncritically adhered to by the ardent advocates of population control. They refuse to penetrate the deeper issues concerning the mutually contradictory elements in production relations; and they totally ignore the facts of colonial and neo-colonial exploitation. As a result, very often, the bogey of rising population is used to obfuscate the contradictions in society, to create an ideological hegemony justifying the prevailing moribund institutions and the dominant social classes.

## FLAWS OF NEO-MALTHUSIAN THEORY

The aim of this chapter, is to cosider the relevance of the Major propositions concerning the relation between the population and development in the third world. Towards this end, we shall outline in brief the main demographic theories : No attempt is made here to present this in a comprehensive way, as that would be beyond our competence. Our analysis will, thus, confine itself to pointing out some of the crucial flaws in the basic premise of the neo-Mathusian theory, which appear to us to be relevant to a discussion of the relation between population growth and socio-economic progress, especially in the third world.

Let us begin with the popular Malthusian theory on population. Malthus, in his well known "Essay on the Principle of Population" (1978)[1] pointed out the disparity between the growth of the population and the means of subsistence. He observed that, unless otherwise checked, it is the natural tendency of population to increase geometrically by doubling almost every 25 years, whereas food production can at best increase arithmetically at a small constant rate over that produced initially. The discrepancy thus arising, between the means of livelihood and the size of the population, is regulated by means of wars, epidemics, famines, limitation of marriages, birth control, abortion, and other methods of checking the population growth. As a clergyman, he was critical of abortion and the like, and suggested 'moral restraint' and prolonged celibacy coupled with chastity.[2]

Malthus did not substantiate his argument, that the means of subsistence cannot grow as rapidly as the population, or that the latter has the tendency to outstrip the former. He considered mainly the limitation of land supply, and thought that this limitation is eternal and immutable. He failed to foresee the development of technology, extension of cultivable area, international trade, and potential of changing social organisations. In fact, he denied the human potential, and insisted that human intervention is powerless to withstand the inevitability of the nature. Thus, for him, the population problem is essentially, one of the balance between people and resources (mainly land). And, since population grows rapidly over the limited resources, poverty and underdevelopment would

1. T. R. Malthus, "Population : The First Essay" (Ann Arbor : University of Michigan Press, 1959)

2. In this connection, we may remember M. K. Gandhi, who advocated sexual abstinence in marriage to prevent unwanted children. He said, "the union [marriage] is meant not for pleasure but for bringing forth progeny And union is criminal when the desire for progeny is absent." *Young India* March 12, 1925. Today, this restraint is believed untenable.

Table 1

*Area and Population of Different Regions of the World*

(Mid-1971)

| *Regions* | *Area (sq. kms)* | *Population (millions)* | *Number of States and Territories* |
|---|---|---|---|
| Europe | 10,500,000 | 650 | 37 |
| Asia | 44,400,000 | 2160 | 42 |
| Africa | 30,300,000 | 353 | 56 |
| America | 42,100,000 | 522 | 47 |
| Australia and Oceania | 8,500,000 | 20 | 24 |
| Total | 135,800,000 | 3705 | 206 |

*Source* : K. Spidchenko, ' Economic Geography of the World", Moscow : Progress Publisher, 1972, p. 18.

inevitably increase, corresponding to the demographic expansion. In this way, he not only rationalised the existence of the poverty of the masses, but also urged that some (the poor) must perish when population presses beyond subsistence.

Needless to elaborate the character of the Malthusian theory of population. It is a pessimistic, deterministic, theory which attempts to rationalise capitalist and imperialist exploitation. Naturally, it is the most influential theory about population. Several classical and neoclassical economists have admired the theory, with only some minor qualifications. And, as we will soon see, since the time of Malthus, the literature on population has been filled with pessimistic prognostications of the impending shortage of natural resources and foodstuffs. For the time being, let us brief Marx's theory on population which stands quite opposite to Malthus's.

In direct contradiction to the Malthusian 'natural' theory, Marx and Engels insisted that it is impossible to speak of any generally applicable law of population, which is the same for all times and all places.[3] They argued that population processes are

3. The arguments of Karl Marx and Fredrick Engels on population have been reproduced in R.L. Meek (*ed.*) "Marx and Engels on the Population Bomb" (Berkeley, Calif : Ramparts Press, 1971).

**Table 2**

*Number of People in Relation to Tied Acreage (1958-59)*

| *Country* | *No. of People per Acre of Tilled Land* |
|---|---|
| Japan | 7.4 |
| Netherlands | 4.4 |
| Egypt | 3.9 |
| UK | 2.9 |
| China | 2.5 |
| Peru | 2.4 |
| Indonesia | 2.0 |
| Norway | 1.7 |
| Brazil | 1.4 |
| Italy | 1.2 |
| India | 1.1 |
| WORLD | 0.80 |
| Mexico | 0.70 |
| Nigeria | 0.60 |
| US and USSR | 0.38 |
| Argentina | 0.28 |
| Australia and Canada | 0.17 |

*Source* : G. Borgstrom, "The Hungry Planet", New York : The Macmillan Co. 1965, p. 5.

related to the social organisation. Its growth depends on diverse factors—such as the level of productive forces, the relations of production, the state and the laws about morality, political and other ideas, religion, and also the geographical environment. Of-course, ultimately, the relations of production determine the population. Accordingly, each socio-economic formation has its own, historically transient, law of population.

With regard to overpopulation, Marx observed that it is purely relative to a particular set of institutional arrangements in a society, at a particular historical time and space. For instance, in a capitalist society, there is capital accumulation which forces migration of workers and creates relative overpopulation manifested in unemployment. That is to say, overpopulation is built into the very system of capitalism. So a low rate of population growth is no remedy, it is the mode of production that must be changed. He made a distinction between the 'means of subsistence' and the 'means of employment', and observed that poverty is due to the pressure on the means of employment and not on the means of subsistence. By this, he emplied that social relations present a formidable obstacle to the productive use of human resources, and thus create an artificial scarcity of the means of subsistence. This is topical; but after Marx there is hardly any comprehensive attempt to develop the same argument. Moreover, it is only very recently that a few Marxist scholars have taken up the study of population growth. Primarily for that reason, meagre work has been done on population from a Marxist standpoint.

In the absence of decisive works by Marxists, the Malthusians, being encouraged by the imperialist powers, have undertaken various sophisticated researches on population. In changing circumstances, they have modified the original theory, and it is now known as the neo-Malthusian theory. According to this theory, the present unprecedented rate of population growth increasingly presses on limited natural resources, and results in diminishing returns. Therefore, to achieve a given rate of economic growth, an ever-increasing rate of investment becomes necessary. However, since high growth of population means more young dependants on those who are engaged in production, there remain very little savings, which consequently limit the possibility of meeting the demand for higher investment. Thus, ultimately, economic growth and social development are obstructed by the rapid rise of population And, unless this trend is deliberately checked, it contains inevitable danger to human society.

Accordingly, neo-Malthusians argue that population must be proportioned to resources so as to achieve the best economic effect. Here comes the concept of 'optimum population.' This refers to the number of people who, in balance with the available resources and the existing level of technology, would produce the highest

**Table 3**

*Share of Different Regions in Total World Population (1650-1957)*

| Year | World Total | | Africa | | Northern America | | Latin America | | Asia (Excluding USSR) | | Europe and USSR | | Oceania | |
|---|---|---|---|---|---|---|---|---|---|---|---|---|---|---|
| | No. | Per Cent | No. | Per Cent | No. | Per Cent | No. | Per Cent | No. | Per Cent | No. | Per Cent | No. | Per Cent |
| 1650 | 545 | 100.0 | 100 | 18.3 | 1 | 0.2 | 12 | 2.2 | 327 | 60.0 | 103 | 18.9 | 2 | 0.4 |
| 1750 | 728 | 100.0 | 95 | 13.0 | 1 | 0.1 | 11 | 1.5 | 475 | 65.2 | 144 | 19.8 | 2 | 0.3 |
| 1800 | 906 | 100.0 | 90 | 9.9 | 6 | 0.7 | 19 | 2.1 | 597 | 66.9 | 192 | 21.2 | 2 | 0.2 |
| 1850 | 1171 | 100.0 | 95 | 8.1 | 26 | 2.2 | 33 | 2.8 | 741 | 63.3 | 274 | 23.4 | 2 | 0.2 |
| 1900 | 1608 | 100.0 | 120 | 7.5 | 81 | 5.0 | 63 | 3.9 | 915 | 56.9 | 423 | 26.3 | 6 | 0.4 |
| 1920 | 1810 | 100.0 | 140 | 7.7 | 117 | 6.5 | 91 | 5.0 | 967 | 53.4 | 486 | 26.9 | 9 | 0.5 |
| 1930 | 2013 | 100.0 | 155 | 7.7 | 135 | 6.7 | 109 | 5.3 | 1073 | 53.5 | 531 | 26.3 | 10 | 0 5 |
| 1940 | 2046 | 100.0 | 172 | 7.7 | 146 | 6.5 | 131 | 5.8 | 1213 | 54.0 | 572 | 25.5 | 11 | 0.5 |
| 1950 | 2495 | 100.0 | 199 | 8.0 | 168 | 6.7 | 162 | 6.5 | 1379 | 55.3 | 574 | 23.0 | 13 | 0.5 |
| 1957 | 2795 | 100.0 | 225 | 8.0 | 189 | 6.8 | 192 | 6.9 | 1556 | 55.7 | 618 | 22.1 | 15 | 0.5 |

*Source* : 1650-1850 estimates from "Determinants and Consequences of Population Trends", United Nations, 1953, Table 2, p. 11. The figures represent United Nations Adjustments of A. M. Carr-Saunders' estimates. See his, "World Population : Past Growth and Present Trends" London, 1936, p. 42. 1900-1950 estimates from United Nations," Demogrphic Year Book, 1957," Table 2, p. 123; those for 1957 are from "Demographic Year Book, 1958", p. 1040.

level of living. Based on this concept, are popular terms such as 'overpopulation' and 'underpopulation'. What is more, all these terms are used in a way that suggests they are self-explanatory and have some absolute significance. The fact that these are absolutely relative to a specific time, space, and purpose, is often ignored.

With the help of selective statistical data, neo-Malthusian's attempt to demonstrate the adverse effects of population growth on investment, output, and capital-output ratio.[4] Their primary focus is explanation of the poverty and the underdevelopment of third world countries which together threaten the basis of the existing political order. The explanation is done in terms of overpopulation and follow-ups. Following from this mission, we have inherited a massive literature.

The popular proposition explaining the underdevelopment of the third world is that the population in the third world has become —or is becoming—too large in relation to the available resources, i.e., that the third world is overpopulated; and that the present high rate of population growth is the main (perhaps the only) obstacle to the socio-economic development of third world countries.

Several questions emerge from the above propostion. Are the countries in the third world overpopulated ? Are the resources estimated so as to bring a correlation between the size of the population and the available resources ? Are the known resources handled solely for the betterment of the third world masses ? Is it not possible to efiect social development by discovery of new resources, better exploitation of existing resources, technological invention, and changes in social system ? Do we not also have evidence that, in a higher density of population the standard of living is higher than what it used to be in a lower density of population? Is there any guarantee that a low rate of growth of population would increase investment capacity ? And finally, without changing the social organisation, would the decrease in the population growth alone help socio-economic progress in the third world ? Let us try to answer these and other questions in the following.

4. For a discussion see, J. Tinbergen, "The Design of Development" (Baltimore : Johns Hopkins Press, 1958), Chap. I.

**Table 4**

*Annual Rate of Growth of Population and Per Capita Income in Some Underdeveloped Countries*

| *Location* | *Annual Rate of Growth* | |
|---|---|---|
| | *Population in 1969* | *Per Capita Income 1957-59 to 1964-66* |
| Morocco | 3.0 | 0.2 |
| Mozambique | 1.2 | 2.9 |
| Nigeria | 2.5 | 3.2 |
| Uganda | 2.5 | 1.2 |
| Sudan | 3.0 | 1.7 |
| Domanican Republic | 3.4 | —0.6 |
| El Salvador | 3.3 | 2.5 |
| Panama | 3.2 | 4.2 |
| Bolivia | 2.4 | 2.8 |
| Brazil | 2.8 | 1.9 |
| Chile | 2.3 | 2.3 |
| Colombia | 3.4 | 1.4 |
| Peru | 3.1 | 3.5 |
| Iran | 3.1 | 3.7 |
| Iraq | 2.5 | 4.2 |
| Burma | 2.2 | 1.5 |
| India | 2.5 | 1.7 |
| Pakistan | 3.3 | 2.8 |
| S. Korea | 2.8 | 3.2 |
| Malaysia | 3.1 | 2.8 |
| Philippines | 3.5 | 0.9 |
| Thailand | 3.1 | 4.2 |

*Source :* Column 1 from "1969 World Population Data Sheet", Population Reference Bureau, Washington D.C; Column 2 from "National Accounts of Less-Developed Countries" Development Centre, OECD, Paris, July, 1968.

Contrary to the belief that the third world is overpopulated (or becoming overpopulated), there are several very sparsely populated countries in Africa, Latin America, and also in some parts of Asia, which—even if their present rate of growth of population is above two per cent—will not reach the density of the capitalist world for a long time. For example, Africa is almost three times as large as Europe, yet its population is approximately 50 per cent smaller than that of Europe (Table 1). However, prior to the advent of colonialism in Africa and the growth of slave trade—through which about 100 million Africans were turned into slaves—the population of Africa was even bigger than that of Europe.

Admittedly, the rate of growth of population is slow in the capitalistic countries but many of them are already densely populated. In this context, a comparison between some of the highly populated countries of Europe and Asia—representing the first and the third world respectively—may reveal the point further. The density per sq. km. in 1972 for England and Wales was 324, for Netherlands 319, for Belgium 317, for Japan 280, for the Federal Republic of Germany 240, and for Italy 178, on the other hand, for Bangladesh it was 425, for India it was 164, for the Philipines 123, for Indonesia 81, and for Pakistan 67.[5] Thus, excluding Bangladesh, all the other mentioned third world countries are 'less populated' than the capitalist countries. In fact, it is not the third world but the first world which is overpopulated.

Now, let us also consider the density of population over useable land. For, one may argue that having more space need not mean that the total space is habitable or useful for cultivation. But we also know that not more than 10 per cent of the total land in the third world is under cultivation and that considerable reserves of arable land remain unused. Anyway, even if we take up the

5. See E. Hofsten, "The Family Planning Controversy", *Monthly Review*, vol. 26, no. 6 (Nov. 1974) p. 19. Table 1 shows that Europe is the most heavily populated part of the world. Even in 1950, the population density of Europe was 80 persons per sq. km. as compared with 57 persons for Asia. Kuan-I Chen, "World Population Growth and Living Standards" (New York : Bookman Associates, 1960), p. 47.

density on tilled acreage, the third world countries do not compare badly with Japan, Netherlands, and even UK (Table 2). There are several third world countries which have less numbers of people than the world average counts. Another estimate is that, in Japan there are nine persons per cultivated acre, in Britain five, while in India there are two.[6] We should also remember that we have much more cultivable land, remaining waste, compared with the Western world.

Besides land, there is the question of mineral and other resources. Whether the third world has inadequate resources to meet its size of population, is thus the next pertinent question. The problem of resource is a relative one. Resources are never fixed, except for the short run; over time, they expand with social development and development of knowledge. Resource exploitation is also a social phenomenon. It is the social structures which determine the importance of the different resources, allocate them and distribute them.

Everywhere in the third world, there are considerable reserves of underground minerals, out of which only a small part have so far been explored. There are also petroleum-rich countries, too, such as Iraq, Iran, Libya, Saudi Arabia, and Kuwait. In addition, there are hundreds of rivers which have never been used for irrigation or for generation of power. Generally speaking, underdeveloped nations are not poor in resources. Nature has distributed its bounties unevenly, and that is to the advantage of the third world. The major problem is of the social relations of production—impending the exploitation of the resources and the distribution of profit. The fact is that natural-patriarchal, feudal and semi-feudal, and petty-commodity production hold back labour productivity. And, taking advantage of the situation, the colonial and imperial powers have drained out and continue to—drain out the resources through several means—and hence perpetuate the underdevelopment of the third world.

6. Refer to D. Wilson, "A Quarter of Mankind" (Penguin Books, 1968), p. 302.

**Table 5**

*Agricultural and Industrial Growth in 1960-67*

| *Region* | *Average Annual Increase* | |
|---|---|---|
| | *Agriculture* | *Industry* |
| Capitalist World | 3.0 | 6.0 |
| Socialist World | 3.5 | 8.5 |
| Third World | 2.1 | 6.5 |
| Whole World | 2.7 | 6.5 |

*Source* : "World Economic Survey, 1968", United Nations.

To recapitulate the foregoing. The third world is not over-populated, rather many of its countries can safely accomodate a larger population than at present.[7] As for resources, their little-explored underground wealth is in no way less than that of the other worlds. But it is because of colonialism and imperialism, on the one hand and internal production relations, on the other, that the potentiality for capital investment and economic growth is restricted today. In short, the third world is underdeveloped, not because of the size of its populations or because of less resources, but because of the existing relations of production. No doubt, some cities of the third world—such as Jakarta, Calcutta, Sao Paulo, Port Harcourt, etc.—have relatively higher populations, manifested in unemployment, slums, etc. But even this is largely because of the type of economic system which has forced extensive rural migration to the towns.

Further, in the light of the deversity of demography, resources, political economy, and socio-cultural organisations among the third world countries, the general neo-Malthusian explanation for underdevelopment as being due to overpopulation, cannot stand. The term 'over population' seems popular because, with it, all vital problems like poverty, unemployment, and many other such phenomena, can be so glibly explained. Thereby, attention can be diverted from the real causes of backwardness. In this way the

7. See, E. Boserup, "The Conditions for Agricultural Growth" (London : Allen and Unwin, 1965).

**Table 6**

*Growth of Gross Domestic Product, 1950-67*

(1950=100)

| *Year* | *Ceylon* | *Chile* | *Egypt* | *India* | *Taiwan* | *Pakistan* |
|---|---|---|---|---|---|---|
| 1950 | 100.0 | 100.0 | 100.0 | 100.0 | 100.0 | 100.0 |
| 1955 | 121.4 | 116.4 | 123.7 | 118.1 | 150.8 | 109.7 |
| 1960 | 142.6 | 140.8 | 170.0 | 144.0 | 209.2 | 130.6 |
| 1965 | 164.1 | 179.9 | 223.5 | 167.7 | 339.7 | 172.2 |
| 1968 | 189.2 | 261.0 | — | 197.1 | 450.3 | 205.7 |

*Source :* Excerpted from A Maddison, "Economic Progress and Policy in Developing Countries," U.P. 1970, Appendix B.

troubled States of the third world can be saved, where the multinationals have invested millions of dollars and are earning enormous profits every year.

The advocates of population control argue that the high rate of population growth in the third world limits the capacity for savings and investment. In other words, the rapid rise in population is the chief obstacle to the socio-economic development of the third world. But history has something else to say. Increased population growth had been, in fact, one of the prime causes of the rapid economic progress of Europe and North America, over the last 200 years. Whitehead observed that in Western Europe, "a persistently increasing population has been accompanied by an equally persistent rise in the general standard of life."[8] Some authors also hold the same argument for China and India.[9] These Asian countries have the culture and civilisation going back over 2,000 years. At that time too, their most fertile lands were highly populated. Rightly, Boserup has argued that population pressure has been historically a favourable element in the intensification of agriculture—a condition for increased productivity.[10] Similarly

8. A. N. Whitehead, "Adventures of Ideas" (New York : Macmillan), p. 94.

9. For instance, See, F. L. Patton, "Diminishing Returns in Agriculture" (New York : Columbia University Press, 1926), pp. 17, 78.

10. E. Boserup, 1965, *op. cit.*

both Marxist and non-Marxist scholars have argued that people are needed to consume products, so that a small consuming population is actually as impediment to the functioning of the capitalist system.[11]

In any case, the high rate of population growth in the third world has been concluded from a short period of time. Any analysis over a long period (1650-1957) will reveal that their share in world population is lower by almost 10 per cent (Table 3). Besides, between 1650-1957, the population in Africa grew only 2½ times and in Asia (excluding USSR) 4½ times. On the other hand, in Northern America it was 189 times higher, and in Europe (including USSR) 6 times higher. Obviously, the growth of population in the third world has been smaller compared with that in the developed world. As for birth rate, it is only recently that a few of the third world countries have had a birth rate of over 3 per cent; whereas, as early as in 1880 England had a birth rate of 3.4 per cent, and the same trend was noticed in Germany as late as in 1904. In 1931, the Japanese birth rate was more than 3.2.[12] Clearly, than, actual growth of population in the third world is less than that of Europe. And there is no historical evidence that a high density of population was the force inhibiting development.

There is also no evidence that a smaller population would bring prosperity. We may rather notice cases supporting the reverse. Several countries in Africa and Latin America are underpopulated, but they are also underdeveloped. In contrast, densely populated countries like Netherlands, Japan, West Germany, Great Britain, Belgium, Italy, Israel and Czechoslovakia, are highly developed.[13]

11. For example, J. M. Keynes said that the decline of the birth rate in 1920s was the main reason for the depression. P.M. Sweezy argued that in the capitalist system, a slower rate of growth of population can lead to more unemployment. See his, "Theories of Capitalist Development" (New York : 1942).

12. See, E F. Penrose, "Population Theories and Their Application" (Westport : Greenwood Press, 1973), p. 99.

13. See, B. Berelson (*ed.*) "Population Policy in Developed Countries" (New York : McGraw-Hill, 1974), Table 1, p. 3.

**Table 7**

*Functional Distribution of Foreign Assistance for Family Planning Programmes*

| *Functional Activity* | *Percentage of Each Activity Financed by Foreign Assistance* | | | | |
|---|---|---|---|---|---|
| | *India* 1968-69 | *Jamaica* 1969-70 | *Korea* 1968 | *Malaysia* 1969 | *Pakistan* 1968-69 |
| Training | 68 | 77 | 99 | 47 (Training and Information and education combined) | 94 |
| Information and education | 38 | 35 | 75 | | 38 |
| Contraceptive supplies | 40 | 60 | 21 | 94 | 75 |
| Research and evaluation | 28 | 85 | 89 | 52 | 78 |
| Operational activity | 34 | 29 | 38 | 0.7 | 62 |

*Source :* "Questionnaire in National Family Planniag Programmes", OECD Development Centre, 1969.

Let us take a concrete case of the impact of depopulation. In the 16th century,[14] the rich Congo kingdom had a population of about two million. During the colonial period, due to slave trade, emigrant labour, and compulsory military service, Congo's population was reduced to almost a third. Even now, it is yet to reach the 16th century figure. With depopulation, the once prosperous kingdom was ruined and became one of the most backward countries in the world. Its people suffered from chronic food shortage and frequent famines. One may cite several such instances.[15] The arguments about the relation between population growth and underdevelopment are, therefore, very simplistic, and the third world intellectuals have also accepted them uncritically.

14. S. Axelson, "Culture Confrontation in the Lower Congo" (Uppsala, 1970), p. 91.

15. In the history of mankind several dreadful famines, epidemics and wars had occured, each taking away lives of millions of people and ravaging the economy and society. We have also cases inside third world countries of the highly developed regions being densely populated while the sparsely populated areas are less developed. (For instance, in India Jharkhand and the North Eastern Region versus the Peninsula.)

By stressing the adverse impact of a high rate of population growth, the present-day demographers have created undue panic about shortages of foodstuffs in the world—although. over the last 30 years, food production has increased by 50 per cent while world population has gone up by only 35 per cent.[16] This means that there has been an overall increase of 15 per cent in food production.

There is neither causal nor concomitant connection between population growth and per capita income. There are several third world countries—like Nigeria, Panama, Bolivia, Peru, Iraq, Iran, S. Korea and Thailand—who have high rate of annual population growth accompanied by a high rate of growth in per capita income (Table 4). Moreover the third world, as a whole, has a higher rate of annual industrial growth than the capitalist world (Table 5). There are some countries in the third world, which have a very high rate of increase in GNP.[17] Many countries have far higher growth rate of Gross Domestic Product than their population growth rate. Between 1950-65, Ceylon's GDP increased by 64 per cent, Chile's by 80 per cent, Egypt's by 113 per cent, India's by 67 per cent, Taiwan's by 240 per cent, Pakistan's by 72 per cent, etc. (Table 6). Reality does not quite subscribe to the popular neo-Malthusian fear.

The ideological content of birth control becomes more clear, from the role of imperialist powers—especially US which has played a dominant role in publicising the scare of demographic expansion. All along, the major American foundations and the IPPF have generously provided more than half the total resources which have

16. See, Idris Cox, "The Hungry Half" (London : Lawrence and Wishart, 1970), p. 71.

17. For instance, during 1960-67, the annual percentage increase was 19 2 for Libya, 10.0 for Taiwan, 8.8 for Jordan, 7.9 for Iran, 7.6 for South Korea, 7.5 for Ivory Coast and Nicaragua and 6.9 for Iraq. See E.M. Martin, "Development Aid : Successes and Failures" in OECD *Observer*, No. 43, (December 1969), pp. 5-12; see also, G. Ohlin, "Population Control and Economic Development", Development Centre, OECD, Paris, 1967.

gone into the field of family planning in the third world.[18] Total foreign assistance for overseas family planning in 1962 was less than $ 7 million; by 1969, this had increased to about $ 115 million.[19] These figures exclude the US assistance in local currencies generated by food aid. In 1969, the contribution to family planning in the third world from US AID was $ 48 million, of Ford Foundation $ 18 million, of Population Council $ 12.5 million, of SIDA $ 9 million, of IPPF $ 8.4 million, of the Rockefeller Foundation $ 4.5 million, and others a little more than $ 10 million.[20] Foreign assistance for research and training in the family planning programme in the third world countries accounts for a very decisive proportion (for details see Table 7).

One asks why the US, its multinational foundations, and US-dominated world bodies such as the World Bank,[21] carry out a campaign for population control with such crusading zeal. Foreign aid is not charity. It is good business, and contributes to political stability in the recipient countries. The attempts are to create a new smoke-screen in the campaign of exploitation of the third world.[22] Somehow, the third world has accepted the ideological

18. In some countries it is even more than half. For instance in 1968 the percentage of foreign aid for family planning was 68 in Pakistan, 75 in Mauritius, etc. See "Population Programme and Economic and Social Development", Development Centre Studies, OECD 1970, p. 47.

19. *Ibid*, p. 48.

20. There are 11 Western countries (Belgium, Denmark, Finland, Germany, Japan, Netherlands, Norway, Sweeden, Switzerland, U.K. and USA), some multilateral agencies (UN, WHO, UNICEF, ILO, FAO, UNESCO, IBRD, OAS, OECD and Colombo Plan) and private foundations and organisations (21 of USA, 4 of England, and one of Japan) which have been active in the birth control and family planning programmes of the third world.

21. In his initial speeches president of World Bank, R. S. McNamara insisted that rapid population increase is "one of the greatest barriers to the economic growth and social well-being of our member states." See his "Address to the Board of Governors, World Bank," *Population Bulletin* 24, no. 3 (Nov. 1968), pp. 69-70.

22. For an instance of intensity of imperialist exploitation we may mention a World Bank estimate which found that the net flow of private investments into the third world between 1960 and 1968 was roughly £13,000 million earning a profit of £2,000 million each year. See I Cox, 1970, *op, cit.* p. 46.

hegemony which covers exploitation by the multinationals and safeguards the decaying internal social institutions of the third world countries. Indeed, the so-called, experts of the third world are trailing behind the guides and mentors of Princeton, Michigan, Harvard, Berkeley, Boston, and other centres for population studies in the US, which have influenced the course of population policy. The foreign agencies have also penetrated into the third world countries, in the garb of guiding some US-bred policies such as Community Development, Green Revolution, birth control, etc. They have thereby even managed to thwart the internal Processes of social transformation Through these ways they are also attempting to hide the wounds inflicted by colonial and neo-colonial exploitation.

The greatest obstacle to the development of the third world countries lies, in fact, in their dependence on the Western developed countries and their own oppressive socio-economic systems. Their backwardness is not the result of the high rate of population growth but of colonial[23] and neo-colonial exploitation, indigenous archaic modes coupled with feudal, semi-feudal[24] and bureaucratic capital formations. The population problem is basically part of the general socio-economic crisis, caused by the extremely unjust world economy and the internal inequities of the ossified social system. Thus, not population control, but fundamental social transformation, are the essential conditions for achieving a breakthrough in the third world's underdevelopment.

The above arguments do not, however, belittle the significance of population policies. In a planned economy and society, it is an essential requirement so far as the improvement of the conditions of life and work of the entire population is concerned. The general health of the mother and children shall be looked after. In that concern, attempts must be made to implement, certain policies for

23. See, Josue de Castro, "Geography of Hunger" (London, 1952).

24. Even World Bank has accepted that the Socio-economic system operating in the countryside is generally hindering the rural development process. "The Assault on World Poverty, Problems of Rural Development, Education and Health". A World Bank Publication, 1975, p. 21.

raising the marriageable age, and to propagate the importance of having gaps between child bearings and opting for planned families. But population control is not the precursor of socio-economic development as is often believed. Population control can achieve little in isolation from the structural transformation. And so, one must see the structural constraints Some economies may need large families,[25] and similarly a proper consideration may have to be given to the sparsely populated regions and communities.[26] Moreover, before introducing any stric objectives in the population policies of the third world, it is necessary to fulfil the minimal human requirements.[27] Our arguments only imply that consideration of population, in isolation from imperialist domination and internal production relations, is insufficient. It side-tracks the fundamental causes of backwardness of third world countries.[28]

To reprise the main findings of the foregoing discussion, we may note that there is no strong correlation between the high rate of population growth and the underdevelopment of these societies,

25. In subsistence types of agriculture, people are convinced that more children are to their benefit. They are also necessary for looking after the parents in their old age. Moreover, in the face of high infant mortality and diseases, people opt for more children. See in this context, M. Mamdani "The Myth of Population Control : Family, Caste, Class in an Indian Village" (New York : Monthly Review Press, 1972) See also L. Pearson, Partners in Development" (Pall Mall Press, 1969), pp. 197-98

26. For instance in India (1961) density of population varied from 155 per sq. km. in Assam and 189 in MP to 1.032 in West Bengal and 1,127 in Kerala. Similar disparities are also observed between districts, and with regard to the birth rate. See G. Chand, "Population in Perspective" (New Delhi ; Orient Longman Ltd., 1972), p. 127. About communities, there are several small tribal and other communities which need more population to safeguard their interests.

27. In this context, it may be useful to study the Chinese experience. See, Chen Pi-Chao, "China's Population Programme at the Grass-Roots Level," *Studies in Family Planning* (August 1973).

28. On India, D. Banerji observes that the bogey of rising population came in very handy for covering up the massive failures of the government and "side-tracked the basic problems of poverty, social injustice, ill health, primary education and illiteracy, . . .", 'Strategy for Family Planning", *Social Scientist*, Vol. 1, No. 1 (August (1972), p. 42.

Rather, history has provided evidences in reverse. Again, the popular belief that the third world is over populated appears untrue. The present high birth rate is not unique to the third world. Western Europe had already experienced it.

Thus the major cause of underdevelopment of the world is not the size of population, but the colonial and neo-colonial exploitation and the pre-capitalist social formations. To cover the fact of such exploitation, imperialist agencies are trying their best to put the blame on the growth of population. This, however, does not mean that population policies are not necessary. These should mainly concern themselves with the improvement of conditions of life and work of the entire population, giving particular emphasis to the health of mothers and children. The path for the development of the third world, thus, lies through its structural transformations to release its own productive forces and through continuous struggles against the external exploitative and reactionary forces.

[The author is grateful to Suguna Paul, Manu Bhaskar, TG. Jacob and D. R. K. Reddy for help. However, the views expressed are those of the author.]

# 9

# NEW TRENDS IN ANTHROPOLOGY

## AREAS OF CONVERGENCE

FOLLOWING the disintegration of colonialism, shift of power from Western Europe to the United States of America, emergence of anti-imperialist struggles in the Third World, unprecedented rise of unemployment and inflation and rapid growth of both escapist and rebellious tendencies in the capitalist countries, together tended to erode the basic premises, assumptions and presuppositions of the conventional British school of structural-functional Anthropology. Modes and categories of a structural functionalism no longer appeared to fit the reality experienced by the different societies. The inherited emphasis on consensus, harmony and integration were plainly found inappropriate and politically biased in favour of the dominants. The radical social change called for a model which would grasp a complex reality of conflict, oppression and domination. At this juncture, among other models, structuralism was systematically developed in the field of social sciences in the 1960s. Though a relatively young trend of thought, it has become one of the most flourishing theoretical trends in the contemporary Anthropology.

At the same time, the successful socialist revolutions in some precapitalist societies under the leadership of both the peasants and workers instead of the expected success in capitalistic western societies under the leadership of the proletariat, raised fundamental questions in historical materialism. The view of dominance of the economic base and the dependence of the superstructure on the base, and development of society by implacable laws of chronological succession of universal stages inexorably leading to the process of realization of a communist society was found oversimplified in terms of the concrete accumulated experience of the world since the Chinese revolution in the late 1940s. As a consequence, a rethinking of historical materialism was carried out by several eminent scholars. And here, among other trends, the most inspiring was the development of neo structuralism[1].

In close association with the aforementioned trends, there was a conspicuous development of Marxist economic Anthropology in the 1960s. It marked a complete departure from the previous studies of primitive economies. Marxism is reinterpreted through structuralism. The trend is both an extension of structuralism and Marxism, and an attempted synthesis of the two.

This Book intends to consider the simultaneous rise of the three trends with their salient points of association enriching one another, specially Marxist economic Anthropology. Within each trend there have been several variations, which obviously cannot be treated here, in any detail. We are interested only in locating the broad area of convergence between them. Besides, the Book primarily deals with the acknowledged authorities in the respective fields—Claude Levi-Strauss on structuralism, Louis Althusser on neo structuralism, and Maurice Godelier and Claude Meillassoux on Marxist economic Anthropolog .

## STRUCTURALISM

The original ideas of structuralism can be traced in the works of some mathematicians, linguists and psychologists in the early twenteeth century[2]. They conceived structure as immutable despite the continued alteration of its parts and the whole itself, and changes only when the whole undergoes a qualitative leap. On the other hand, all the elements of the whole are essentially dependent on its structure. Hence, it was considered necessary to study the

1. J. Pathy, "Towards an Appraisal of Historical Materialism", *Society and Change*, 1 (3) 1980, pp. 201-218.

2. A. Podgorecki and M. Loas, *Multi-Dimensional Sociology*, Routledge and Kegan Paul, London 1979, pp. 31-41.

structure of an object before the study of its elements and parts.

But the systematic presentation of structuralism in the field of social sciences began with the works of Claude Levi-Strauss and Michael Foucault, and in a sense, the former alone played a decisive role in popularising structuralism in Anthropology. Unlike the British school of social anthropology, which considers structure as the institutionalized structure of observable relations between individuals, Levi-Strauss views structure as an underlying set of structural elements with their rules of combination and opposition, from which the complete range of possible forms of such relations can be generated. He insists that empirical relations can be explained as the manifestation of a hidden infrastructure which can only be reconstructed through theoretical effort.

In other words, structure is never directly decipherable at the empirical level, though it constitutes a level of reality behind the visible social relations, and that can be discovered only through models and hypotheses[3]. "Structure, in this terms, is the syntax of transformation which never exists in empirical form itself, but empirically existing phenomena are to be seen as different combinations and permutations of the same elements"[4].

The main task of structuralist analysis therefore consists in locating the essential relationships between some identifiable elements within the given whole. These objective relationships explain the totality and also determine the roles of its parts and their patterned combinations. To quote Levi-Strauss, in this connection, the method of structuralist analysis ". . . consists in the following operations : (1) define the phenomenon under study as a relation between two or more terms, real or supposed ; (2) construct a table of possible permutations between these terms; (3) take this table as the general object of analysis which, at this level only, can yield necessary connections, the empirical phenomenon considered at

3. C. Levi-Strauss, *Structural Anthropology*, Allen Lane, London 1968, ch. XV.

4. M. Glucksmann, *Structurallst Analysis in Contemporary Thought : A Comparison of the Theories of C. Levi-Strauss nda L. Althusser*, Routledge and Kegan Paul, London 1974, p. 163.

the beginning being only one possible combination among others, the complete system of which must be reconstructed beforehand."[5]

**Structural Analysis**

Further, Levi-Strauss argues at length that social realities are historically general. Various situations in the different historical epochs are primarily characterised by varied configurations of given elements, in relation to the current system of elements. Thus diachronic and synchronic analyses are simply two variants of the structural analysis.[6] He further argues that the notion of historical progress is simply a myth, as historical change is nothing more than variation within a structure of cultural possibilities whose underlying assumptions remain unchanged.

In brief, the fundamental features of structuralism in terms of which Levi-Strauss has analysed the systems of kinship, myth and others are : (a) the rejection of empiricist analysis in favour of scientific study of the objective structures; (b) the formulation of a series of discrete levels and elements and a limited number of key combinatory principles through which the empirical permutations of the system can be reconstructed; and (c) the rejection of historical analysis in favour of synchronic reality.

Applying the above principles of structuralism, Levi-Strauss advances a number of startling conclusions like :

(1) The elements and developments of a social phenomenon acquire meaning only as aspects of a definite totality, as elements of a specific system, and hence, the analysis of the structures of social phenomenon is the *sine qua non* for understanding society. And a scientific research necessarily means discovering the basic and universal structural elements of all human societies.

(2) Since all cultures are the products of human brains, there must be common universal features somewhere beneath the surface, at the level of structure which one can never notice at the level of manifest fact.[7] The concealment is due to the nature of

5. C. Levi-Strauss, *Totemism*, Beacon Press, Boston 1963, p. 16.

6. C. Levi-Strauss, *The Savage Mind*, Weidenfeld and Nicolson, London 1974, p. 256.

7. E. Leach, *Levi-Strauss*, Fontana, London 1970, pp. 21-36.

structure itself and has nothing to do with the level of consciousness. The variations in the cultural patterns is only a variation in the means of expression of the unconscious mind projected onto symbolic interaction in all its forms. Hence, the distinction between 'primitive' and 'modern' are objectively unfounded.

While there would be little dispute on the significance of examining the different social structures and their components in their unity and diversity, his generalisations on universal structure of culture intentionally reflects a form of extreme psychological reductionism and profound anti-historicism. The model evading history fails to locate the determinants of the diverse forms of social structure and is divorced far away from explaining the social transformations from one structure to another.

## NEO STRUCTURALISM

Neo structuralism refers to the body of theoretical work produced since the late 1960s by Louis Althusser, Etienne Balibar, Nicos Poulantzas, and some Marxist anthropologists. There are enough differences, but in common they share a structuralist interpretation of the works of Karl Marx. Althusser is the leading architect of this school.

Althusser argues that most of the commentators on Marx have provided a humanist and historicist interpretation mainly basing on Marx's early philosophical writings. He locates radical "epistemological break" in 1845 with *Capital*, a break from humanist and historicist philosophy to a scientific, objective structural analysis of the economic context. He seeks to establish the scientificity of Marx's thought and to distinguish it from all varieties of humanism and historicism.

The neo structuralists in common hold that the concept of mode of production is an abstract object referring to a matrix of structures, institutions and relationships. The social formations (societies) are only the concrete forms observable in historical societies. These formations are naturally innumerable while the concept of 'modes', being ideal and analytical categories, are few.

These forms can be understood from an *a priori* valid axiom of modes of production which must be empirically verified in each case. Most social formations possess a class structure that results from the articulation or combination of two or more modes of production, one of which is dominant at any given moment, and the other(s) subordinate. The specific modes and the concrete form in which they are combined, determine the character of the classes in the social formation.[8]

Social formations consist of many overlapping and intersecting structures, invariably comprising distinct and relatively autonomous economic, political, and in ideological structures. This complex totality is interrelated and structured through the relations of dominance and determinance : among the various structural 'instances', one 'instance' will have the dominant role, varying according to the social formation, and yet, in all cases, its role is determined in the last instance by the economy.

**Ambiguous Alternative**

The relative autonomy of the superstructures and their specific effectiveness and the determination in-the-last-instance by the economic together "constitutes the essence of any social formation."[9] In other words, economy has a critical influence but its influence is mediated in and by different forms through different structures. This was however, already dormant in Engels' references to the relative autonomy of superstructures *vis-a-vis* economic conditions. All that Althusser succeeds in doing is to replace the specific problem of economic determinism by an ambiguous alternative in which all the elements of structure and superstructure are interrelated in terms of the ultimately economic.[10] The elements of vagueness in the determination of superstructure by base remain as before through the lavish use of "relative autonomy" and

8. N. Poulantzas, *Political Power and Social Classes*, New Left Books, London 1973, pp. 70-73.

9. L. Althusser, *For Marx*, Allen Lane, London 1969, p. 111.

10. L. Kolakowski, "Althusser's Marx" *The Socialist Register*, The Merlin Press, London 1971, pp. 111-128.

"in the last instance." He too did not say what he meant by the last instance and did never attempt to explore what determines what, and under what circumstances.

Anyway, in the structural complex unity is arrived at through the contradictions articulated in dominance and governed by the laws of uneven development. The contradictions are of various types. In any given complex unit, there would be one principal contradiction and there is a principal aspect in every contradiction. Thus social structure is characterised by the domination—subordination relations between the contradictions and between their aspects. The multidimensional causality of a structure contains quasiautonomous and simultaneously interrelated substructure and their elements reflecting differential degree of causal influence upon one another and on the totality itself. Hence, there is "over-determination" which, however, theoretically explores little.

Naturally, like Levi-strauss, Althusser is very critical of empiricism. For him, it means a certain theory of knowledge which claims that knowing consists in extracting from the real object, a pre-existing "essence" included and blurred by external appearances.[11] He remarks that knowledge has nothing to do with "empiricist" ideology but with abstractions which are already elaborated and conceptualized.[12] All neo structuralists are committed to the reality of invisible underlying structures. Though the ubiquity of contradictions within and in between structural elements and structures are asserted, their actual necessity is never demonstrated.

## Man in History

Like structuralists who rejected the anthropological notion of individuals as the subjects or agents of history and treated the individuals as the simple bearers of the structural relations within which they are situated, the neostructuralists have also rejected

11. L. Althusser and E. Balibar, *Reading Capital*, New Left Books, London 1970, p. 35.

12. L. Althusser, *op cit.*, p. 183.

the human subject as the basis from which to construct a scientific understanding of society.

> The structure of the relations of production determines the places and functions occupied and adopted by the agents of production who are never anything more than the occupants of these places, in so far as they are the 'supports' of those functions.[13]

For neostructuralists, scientific Marxism contains not men and men's conscious action, but the social structures and social formations that invisibly move them and shape history. Such an outright rejection of the active and creative role of man in history, the denial of *praxis*, naturally inhibits construction of a relevant theory of revolutionary struggles.

Incidentally, the remark of Marx that men make their own history but not in freely chosen circumstances, dates from 1852, after the supposed "epistemological break." It was therefore wrong to attribute to Marx that in his later writings he had not considered human beings as the subject of economic process but the distribution of roles and functions in production.[14]

Also like structuralists, the neostructuralists subordinate the historical analysis of social relation to the study of their functional determination within a given social formation. They have denied the significance of the theory of historical transition based on different class struggles in different societies. They argue that the phenomena of genesis and transformation can automatically be deduced from the basic structure of a given social formation. Invariably, the insist on the precedence of structural analysis over historical analysis. Besides, the treatment of causality at the synchronic level, rules out historicism as a method of analysis. The social formation "depends on the conjuncture of a formation in its historical individuality, original in every case."[15]

In short, the common grounds for meeting of structuralism

13. L. Althusser and E. Balibar, *op cit.*, p. 180.
14. *Ibid.*, 160-180.
15. N. Poulantzas, *op cit.*, p. 169.

and neostructuralism are among others, the opposition to empiricism, humanism and historicism. Althusser in particular can also be credited for managing to combine Levi-Strauss with Sociology and reintroducing Sociology into Marxism.

Since the mid-1960s, there has been a considerable dialogue between structuralism and Marxism, mainly through certain theoretical categories like "mode of production", "social farmation", "reproduction", and "articulation". The attempts to reformulate Marxist theory are, however, motivated to overcome the limitations of the orthodox and Hegelian Marxism, and to present Marxism as a more scientific and politically relevant theory of society through the basic tenets of the structuralist method.

Marxism does not deny the significance of examining the different social structures and their components in their unity and diversity. Marx always held that the understanding of social structure is necessary to analyse the progress of society. "It is always the direct relationship of the owners of the conditions of production to the direct producers. . .which reveals the innermost secret—the hidden basis of the entire social structure'.[16]

## STRUCTURALISM AND MARXISM

On several fundamental points, structuralism aad Marxism appear diametrically opposed to each other, especially with regard to the treatment of history and *praxis*. With some obscure analysis, Althusser says that Marx was basically a structuralist and considered historical analysis as only secondary to the structural. But Marxism considers that towards the understanding of society, both historical and structural analyses are indispensable, inseparable and complimentary to each other[17]. Marx was concerned both with the question of periods of human history and with their negations. The maxim of neostructuralism that structures of society and their contradictions alone determine social outcome is not supported by historical materialism.

Contrary to the rejection of the role of human subjects in

16. K. Marx, *Capital*, III, Progress Publishers, Moscow 1959, p. 772.
17. J. Pathy, *op cit*., pp. 211-213.

neostructuralism, Marxism is concerned with the freedom and self-determination of the individual. For Marx, history was a dialectical unity of three inseparable things: (1) the development in accordance with the objective laws, primarily economic; (2) the corresponding development of consciousness; and (3) the corresponding action expressed in the form of class struggles leading to revolutionary transformations of social formations. No doubt, Marx emphasised objective conditions for a successful revolution, but did not reject the subjective elements, as propogated by the neostructuralist school.

On the above two counts, it is evident that an approchement between structuralism and Marxism is impossible. Reinterpretation of Marxism in the light of structuralist method has ultimately resulted in diluting the essence of historical materialism via an unintelligible model of internal contradictions in social phenomena. Nevertheless, it has to be admitted here that neostructuralism has attracted tremendous interest among the progressive intellectuals of various social science disciplines, especially Anthropology.

Since the beginning of the 1960s, Marxist Anthropology was associated with the names of Claude Meillassoux and Maurice Godelier. Soon several anthropologists like Emmanuel Terray, P.P. Rey, Auge Marc, Barry Hindess, Paul Hirst and others joined them.

## MARXIST ECONOMIC ANTHROPOLOGY

Godelier read the works of Marx in the structuralist fashion and examined the causality between the different structures, and more particularly the causality of the mode of production over the other structures. Like Althusser, he asserts that for Marx the scientific understanding of the system consists in the discovery of internal structure hidden behind its visible functioning, and that Marx proposed "the priority of the study of structures over that of their genesis and evolution."[18] Accordingly he argued that the "study of the internal functioning of a structure must precede and

18. M. Godelier, "Structure and Contradiction in Capital", in R. Blackburn (ed.) *Ideology in Social Sciencès*, Fontana, London 1975, p. 338.

illuminate the study of genesis and evolution."[19] The principle of contradiction—inter-systemic—should be explained through the evolution of structures. The real history consists of moving "from a structural morphology to a structural physiology, that is, to a theory of the conditions and reasons for the shift of the locus of the relations of production".[20]

Godelier insisted on the primacy of theoretical practice in the construction of scientific knowledge. He says :

> What both structuralists and Marxists reject are the empiricist definitions of what constitutes a social structure. For Marx as for Levi-Strauss a structure is not a reality that is directly visible, and so directly observable, but a level of reality that exists beyond the visible relations between men, and the functioning of which constitutes the underlying logic of the system, the subjacent order by which the apparent order is to be explained.[21]

Thus, he suggests that economic anthropologists have to attend to the causality of economic structure and their effect on the development of societies.[22]

Meillassoux has differed from Godelier on the assessment of Levi-Strauss's structuralism. While Godelier considered it as a remarkable scientific advance, Meillassoux called it a mystifying ideology. In his study of Guro, Meillassoux uses the categories of historical materialism. He analyses the modes of production of lineage-based and segmentary societies. Production units enter into the process of production as subjects or as agents; each unit combines factors of production and is thus structured by the totality of the relations between its parts.[23]

19. *Ibid*, p. 343.

20. C. Levi-Strauss, M. Godelier and Auge Marc, "Anthropology, History and Ideology", *Critique of Anthropology 6*, 1976-77.

21. M. Godelier, *Rationality and Irrationality in Economics*, Monthly Review Press, New York 1972, pp. XVIII-XIX.

22. M. Godelier, *Marxist Perspectives in Anthropology*, Cambridge University Press, 1977, p. 17.

23. E. Terray, *Marxism and "Primitive" Societies : Two Studies*, Monthly Review Press, New York 1972, pp. 178-179.

Like Althusser, he also argues that there are no primitive societies, and that those are only distinct social formations with the combination of at least two modes of production, one of which is dominant and the other subordinate. That produces specific effects which account for the concrete form taken on by the juridical, political and ideological superstructure. In short, though he was critical of structuralism, his later works did clearly reflect his closeness with structural Marxism or neostructuralism.[24]

**Affinity**

More than Meillassoux, Terray is greatly influenced by Althusser. On the basis of Meillassoux's study, he showed the merits of the concept of social formation and mode of production in the precapitalist societies.[25] His own work on the genesis of the political system of the Abron kingdom in West Africa, is a much more serious attempt in concrete historical study with the basic concepts and categories of historical materialism.[26] A Maoist during student days, he naturally disliked Levi-Strauss's structuralism. He thought it was a combination of mechanical materialism and Kantian ideology.[27] For P.P. Rey also, structuralism was a method that could offer little in the study of actual ongoing societies. His works reflect the linkage with the revolutionary elements of the society.[28]

In brief, though it is difficult to treat all the Marxist economic anthropologists together, one can unmistakably note that they draw inspiration from neostructuralism. They differed largely with regard to structuralism. But since there is a methodological con-

24. C. Meillassoux, "From Reproduction to Production", *Economy and Society*, (ICI) 1972, pp. 93-105.

25. E. Terray, *op cit.*

26. E. Terray, "Event, Structure and History", in Friedman and Rowlands (eds), *The Evolution of Social Systems*, Duckworth, London 1978.

27. J. S. Kahn and J. R. Llober, "French Marxist Anthropology: Twenty Years After", *The Journal of Peasant Studies*, VIII (1), 1980, pp. 89-90.

28. P. P. Rey, "The Lineage Mode of Production", *Critique of Anthropology*, 1975, pp 27-29.

tinuity between structuralism and neostructuralism, those Marxist economic anthropologists who are critical of structuralism cannot in reality escape from the pitfalls of structuralism. On the whole, in crucial areas like the concept of structure, methods of theoretical abstraction, role of human beings, insignificance of historical analysis and others, there appears a strong affinity between structuralism, neostructuralism and Marxist economic Anthropology. A breakdown in the said relations may usher a radical reorientation in Marxist economic Anthropology, and render it more creative.

# 10

## MARXISM AND THE PRIMITIVE: SOME PRELIMINARY COMMENTS

THE FIRST nine-tenths of human social history is characterized as primitive communal. Anthropologists say that even today a part of the mankind continues to live nearly in that stage. One is thus curious to know how could the primitive communal system survived for such a long time and why did some parts of it disintegrated earlier than the others. And as a corollary, is it justifiable to characterize the people of diverse periods and places under a single undifferentiated term, the primitive? Unfortunately the available answers are far from conclusive. Anthropology, a *de facto* science of the primitive, has either evaded the issues or provided stereotyped and politically convenient explanations. Till very recently, the subject was dominated by the anti-theorists, who considered the use of Marxist theory in primitive societies as an aberration of a few politically oriented anthropologists, and thus questioned their 'objectivity'. Even now, though the situation is slightly different, it is still believed that Marx's theory is inapplicable to primitive or 'a historical' societies.[1] The Marxists too, have more often than not, simply repeated the propositions and the framework outlined by Marx and Engels on the basis of the little available inductive evidence of the time. Some have even reduced all precapitalist production systems to a single structure in which direct producers possess the means of production; of all primitive societies to a knowledge

1. Judith Ennew, 'The Material of Reproduction: Anthropological Views on Historical Materialism,' *Economy and Society*, Vol. VIII, No. 1, pp. 99-124.

of primitive communism.[2] Small wonder Marxism made little inroads into the colonially entrenched discipline of anthropology. Fortuitously, in the last two decades, a small but concerted effort is being made to look afresh the primitive systems from the historical materialist perspective and to rectify the distortions that have crept into the Marxist anthropology. But the task is rather difficult, precisely because no amount of knowledge on any of the contemporary community, even in the remotest parts of the world, would be adequate to reconstruct the pristine primitive context and analyse the forces that were responsible for its transformation. The only alternative appears at the moment is to interpret the archaeological and pre-historic evidence, and supplement it with present empirical investigation. This option, however, has hardly been opted by the concerned scholars. As a result, the whole energy is directed towards the exploration of the relative autonomy of the so-called primitive societies of today, and the ways of articulation of capitalism and imperialism into their matrix. The scope, though important, fails to comprehend the totality of the primitive order and its potentialities of change. This brief paper is confined to a critical examination of the Marxist anthropological literature pertaining to the cognition of the primitive society and its dynamics, and subsequently embarks upon some preliminary comments on them.

## I

The concept of the primitive society ought to mean something different from other social formations. Concurrently, the definition and the denominator should have universal validity. The limit to conceptualization is however in-built. The primitive societies manifest innumerable variations in terms of internal organization ecology, demography, external relations and so on. Lack of adequate relevant information has further accentuated the problem.

More than a century ago, Marx and Engels tried to explore the primitive societies by reflecting on the then unexplored pre-historic periods of Germanic and Slavonic tribal societies. Work of L. Von

2. Barry Hindess and Paul Hirst, *Pre-capitalist Modes of Production*, Routledge & Kegan Paul, London, 1975.

Maurer and Lewis Henry Morgan facilitated and confirmed their major hypotheses. Being aware of their fragmentary knowledge of the primitive society, they did not formulate specific laws of the primitive existence and dynamics. Nonetheless, a cursory glance at their works reveals a number of postulates that can be profitably used to understand primitive forms of societies.

Contrary to the general belief, Marx and Engels were aware of certain critical differences among the primitive societies. At least, two different stages of primitive social development were noted. The first one is called "spontaneous community" marked by shared production and immediate distribution of the product according to need, and the second as "early settled primitive" corresponding to the anthropological term, tribe. This revealed meaningful direction, but so far very little attention is paid to it.[3]

Although Marx and Engels mentioned several attributes of primitive society, such as common name, dialect, mythology and rites, mythical ancestor, endogamy, small size and low level of technology, they emphasized communal ownership as the distinguishing feature. The common ties of blood, language, custom etc. "appears not as the *consequence* but as the *precondition of the joint* (temporary) *appropriation* and *use of the soil*."[4] The individuals being powerless, the social organization contains and represses its members in a dictatorial way. In essence, the communal character appears "as a negative unity in relation to the outside world."[5] The community as a whole controls the allocation and use of the means of production, while each kin-based production unit owns tools and product.

The primitive society is separated from all other societies in terms of the absence of surplus, classes, exploitation and private ownership of property. This is problematic, for the simple reason

3. Maurice Godelier, 'The Concept of Tribe', *Perspective in Marxist Anthropology*, Cambridge University Press, 1977, pp 79-87; Kathleen Gough, 'Modes of Production in Southern India,' *Economic and Political Weekly*, Vol. XV, Annual Number, Feb. 1980, pp. 337-64.

4. Karl Marx Frederick Engels, *Pre-Capitalist Socio-economic Formations*, Progress Publishers, Moscow, 1979, p. 86, Emphases in original.

5. *Ibid.*, p. 89.

that absence of denominator cannot fully comprehend a context. What is needed is to specify what exists and determines the essence of the totality of primitive society. Marx and Engels's notions of personal dependence as opposed to free labour and use value as opposed to exchange value, being positive, are more useful for analytical differentiation than absence of individual ownership.[6]

Meillassoux considers relationship of men to land as crucial to understand the different forms of pre-capitalist societies. In hunting and gathering bands, land is the "subject of labour," while for settled agriculturists land is an "instrument of labour." The first one is egalitarian and unstable with little concern for an ideology of biological reproduction. The second type is lineage society, which produces a kinship ideology. It relies less on the control of the "means of material production" than on the "means of human reproduction," *i.e.*, subsistence and women. He considers demographic expansion as the logical means to face the social security requirements.[7] And, "With the development of exchange and the rise of the market economy, kinship as the main expression of peasant social organisation loses its actuality . . . Land becomes a matter of business transactions, and kin dependents give way to wage earners."[8]

This approach is an important contribution in the right direction. Instead of the absence of private ownership of means of production, the emphasis on relationship between men and land is a welcome departure, within the purview of historical materialism. But this too is not without problems. In the first form of society, since the grouping is stable, relations to land as the determining aspect seems to be an imposition of a negative

6. Claude Meillassoux, 'From Reproduction to Production : A Marxist Approach to Economic Anthropology,' *Economy and Society*, Vol. I, No. 1, February 1972, pp. 93-105.

7. *Ibid*, pp. 97-99 and his 'The Social Organisation of the Peasantry : The Economic Basis of Kinship', *The Journal of Peasant Studies*, Vol. I, No. 1, 1973 ; also in J. D. Seddon (ed.), *Relations of Production : Marxist Approaches to Economic Anthropology*, Frank Cass, London, 1976.

8. Claude Meillassoux, 'The Social Organisation. . .,' *The Journal of Peasant Studies*, Vol. I, No. 1, 1973, pp. 88-89.

category, or at least an unwarranted extension of advanced systems. Likewise is the feature of irrelevance of an ideology of kinship in the band stage. At the same time, the relationship between men and men in the process of production in the first stage of society is left out from the analysis.

Nonetheless, Meillassoux's argument of dynamics of kinship relations with the changes in the men and land relationship is more convincing than the confusing position of kinship as ideology, and kinship as production relations.[9] The latter category of argument may be summed up as that under the primitive mode of production, due to the low level of productive forces, man is helpless before nature, and that this explains the collective forms of labour and communalistic social relations implied in the collective ownership of land and the egalitarian forms of distribution of products.[10] In such societies all roles, including political and economic, appear in the form of kinship roles.[11] That is, kinship in primitive societies is both superstructure and infrastructure.[12] With changes in residential, demographic and sexual relations, kinship relations cease to play the dominant role. The circumstances, then, demand new forms of authority. One wonders in vain, why these kin-related changes appeared in the first place, and how these changes changed production relations. Meillassoux did reject over-emphasis of kinship, but could not radically depart from the orthodox position. True, in lineage systems, kinship is temporarily modified to meet the requirements of production and to cover the superstructural relations. But it does neither determine nor dominate the total social organization of primitive formations.[13]

Besides, the formulation gravitates to the cognition of

9. Maurice Godelier, *Rationality and Irrationality in Economics*, New Left Books, London, 1972 ; Hamza Alavi, 'Peasant Classes and Primordial Loyalties,' *The Journal of Peasant Studies*, Vol. I, No. 1, 1973, pp. 23-62.

10. Emmanuel Terray, *Marxism and "Primitive" Societies : Two Studies*, trans., Mary Klopper, Monthly Review Press, New York, 1972.

11. Hamza Alavi, *op. cit.*, p. 33.

12. Maurice Godelier, 'The Concept of Tribe, *op. cit.*, p. 127.

13. Ernest Gellner, 'The Soviet and the Savage,' *Current Anthropology*, Vol. XVI, 1975, p. 598.

structure, and underplays the internal dynamics of society. Each production unit combines factors of production and is thus structured by the totality of the relations between its parts. And today, there are no primitive societies; there are only distinct social formations with the combination of at least two modes of production, one of which is dominant and the other subordinate.[14] But, at least for analytical purposes, if the natural process of the development of a society is not separated from the impact of exogenous forces, it is difficult to understand not only the pre-historic past but also the relative autonomy of the systems and their independent potentialities.

Consequent upon the problems of using land ownership—control and use—or kin relations to comprehend the totality of diverse primitive social formations, and distinguish them more or less sharply from various advanced social formations, the following seeks to outline some less problematic premises.

The decisive factor in all production systems is man himself; his labour power. This labour process includes the labour proper, the object of labour, and the instrument of labour with which man acts on the object in order to regulate and control the relationship between himself and nature.[15] Labour is thus the primary condition of human existence. Secondly, in the process of production, people are linked together, depend upon one another, and enter into definite relations with one another. In other words, any collective work requires some form of co-operation of labour, however elementary that may be. Different forms of co-operation of labour correspond to different types of production systems. But while all forms of primitive society can be explained in terms of the co-operation of labour existing in that society, this alone seems to be inadequate with reference to the antagonistic socio-economic formations, where labour not only appropriates the nature but also is subjected to social exploitation. Because of appropriation of surplus labour in the class societies, the dimension of conflict is manda-

14. Emmanuel Terray, *op. cit.*, pp. 178-79.

15. Karl Marx, *Capital*, Vol. I, Progress Publishers, Moscow, 1971, pp. 173-74.

tory in the process of production. Though the production can only be carried out with some form of co-operation of labour, in the class societies, there would be an increasing trend of alienation of labour from the process of production. Nevertheless, it is impossible to presume the conflict dimension altogether replacing co-operation of labour.

Accordingly different *forms of co-operation of labour* may reveal the different forms of primitive society. The other social aggregates having co-operation along with various degrees and kinds of conflict of labour would distinguish themselves from primitive societies which are characterized only by co-operation of labour.

The treatment of labour co-operation and conflict together in a single analytical scheme may be objected on methodological grounds. But this problem can be resolved at two interdependent levels : one as a dialectical unity at the level of general human history; and the other as a conceptualization of inherent conflict in the matrix of co-operation of labour itself, *i.e.*, conflict between man and nature, man's existence and his work, and between man and man in the process of production. In this sense both the levels reinforce each other, and therefore, reduce the error in the scheme.

Similarly, a possible criticism may be the failure to distinguish between labour and capital. Whereas labour itself is of co-operation, with relations to capital or other aspects of labour process, it is in conflict in class societies. Hence, the levels being different, it may be argued that conflict dimension cannot form part of co-operation of labour. To an extent, this may be valid; but here it is used only to separate class societies from primitive societies, and not as a means to understand class societies. That is, co-operation of labour is used with specific interest in primitive studies, and thus the scope need not be stretched far beyond its explanatory capacity.

In primitive societies there could be several diverse forms of co-operation of labour. But on the basis of the degree of complexity and permanence of interaction among the working people, the forms of co-operation of labour can be arranged. The first form of co-operation is presumably multiple to meet instinctively the immediate challenges of nature and subsistence. Such a form of co-operation being largely reflexive, is unintegrated and unorganized resulting in a certain degree of looseness in the 'group' of people. The group may be described as a natural community or *band.*

Among other forces, demographic expansion and subsequent fall in the required objects of labour necessitate specification of territorial boundaries of the communities. As a result a certain degree of specialization and a temporary politico-religious authority to protect the territorial community property develop. Such a society may have diverse forms of co-operation of labour, mainly depending on the nature of subsistence. Among the hunters, gatherers and fishing communities, their natural division of labour is partially integrated with reference to subsistence. The relationship is horizontal and specific ; and the co-operation may be called as *restricted simple.* The level of complexity of co-operation is relatively higher in case of hunters than the others. Such a society may be described as a *primitive tribe.*

Among the slash and burn cultivators, the natural division of labour is extended and expressed in several related work teams covering the whole group. Co-operation is regular, consistent and reciprocal but varies in volume as per the work in hand. This form of co-operation may be called as *extended simple,* the basis of *tribe.* The units of production and consumption are homologous and coterminous. Once this sort of co-operation is restricted to kinship units, the co-operation is further regularized and lineage leadership gets established.[16] This form of co-operation of labour may be called *kin based simple co-operation,* and is marked by advanced tribe. Most tribal researches refer to this co-operation, and thus emphasize kinship in all primitive communities. It, however is over-generalized for all the phases of primitive society and history. It needs mention here that the terms, primitive tribe, tribe and advanced tribe, are only used descriptively.

The phases of co-operation of labour in primitive societies are

16. Jaganath Pathy, "An Outline of Modes of Production in Tribal India,' in B. Chaudhuri (ed.), *Tribal Development in India : Problems and Prospects,* Inter India Publications, New Delhi, 1982, p. 34.

however neither universal nor appear in inevitable chronological successions. Besides, to any concrete society more than one form of co-operation may exist, but it is likely that one may be dominant and that can enumerate the basic character of the community. Secondly, with the colonial and capitalist expansion, various forms of labour co-operation are distracted and/or retarded ; or its stage have been skipped ; and thus can be understood only in concrete contexts. In other words, the dialectical unity of natural stages of development of forms of co-operation of labour and the exogenous obtruded process of interaction resulting in multiple forms of co-operation require inductive experience. Thirdly, though the forms of co-operation of labour determine the social and cultural aspects of primitive existence, once they are formed, they constantly interact and influence one another. Hence the relationship is far from mechanical.

## II

The second question that interests us is why and how did these primitive societies became the class societies. Marx, in spite of his limited knowledge of primitive societies, did provide a useful, albeit loosely constructed, framework, which may be a starting point for profitable discussion. In 1858, Marx wrote that when the spontaneously evolved community (band) settles down (tribe), the extent to which it is modified "depends on various external, climatic, geographical, physical etc. conditions as well as on their special natural make-up, their tribal character."[17] But his explanations to the breakdown of primitive society is more or less restricted to only certain sectors and phenomena that contributed to the rise of private ownership of production.

The most significant observation that Marx made is that the disintegration of primitive society was largely the product of the internal forces. He says : "Quite apart from harmful influences coming from without, the community contains destructive elements within itself."[18] There is an inherent dualism, communal and

17. Marx Engels, *Pre-Capitalist. . .Formations, op. cit.*, p 86.
18. *Ibid.*, p. 296.

private ownership and use of property, within the overall communal system of production which, under specific conditions become a source of disintegration. In other words, within the communal milieu, there is an unacknowledged and incipient private dimension. The house and farmyard are owned and used privately, certain vegetables are almost always consumed individually; there is periodic distribution of inalienable and common arable land to individuals' control and use of the production for specific period, *i.e.* communal property but private possession; reservation of a part of the common product for reproduction ; authorization to certain individuals to safeguard common interests; and the like are implicitly in contradiction with the communal set-up. The incipient private dimension of the totality becomes explicit only with population growth, technological advancement, and the consequent development of production, social division of labour and commodity exchange.

Although Marx treated population growth and ecological conditions as important influencing factors in the process of change in primitive society,[19] whenever it was argued that primitive society broke down with population pressure and consequent advancement of technology and intensive use of natural resources.[20] When options like migration and increased reliance on storage of food are exhausted, population pressure tends to develop technology and enhance production. The most favourable situation for this is when the growing population is confined to a restricted area surrounded by inhospitable mountains, deserts or oceans, where people have had no other choice but to adopt new methods of production.[21] According to this argument, the new technology is unlikely to be innovated as long as the population size permits the continued use of a given technology and provides a high output

19. *Ibid.*, p. 67-68.

20. M. J. Harner, 'Population Pressure and the Social Evolutions of Agriculturists,' *South Western Journal of Anthropology*, No. 26, 1970.

21. Ester Boserup, 'Environment, Population and Technology in Primitive Societies,' *Population and Development Review*, Vol. II, No. 1, 1976, pp. 21-36 ; B. J. Price, 'Shifts in Production and Organization,' *Current Anthropology*, Vol. XVIII, No. 2, 1976, pp. 209-33.

per unit of labour input.[22]

Demographic expansion is an important contributory factor in social advancement, but to consider this as the motive force in human history will be an over-simplification. This may stimulate development of instruments and methods of production, but cannot create conditions for their development as a general principle. The sparse world population, say five thousand years back, could have easily lived with their food gathering technology. In specific areas, if it was not possible due to ecological barriers, they would have been either decimated by famine, malnutrition and related diseases and epidemics or carried out long-distance marauding raids or rationalized death before or after birth. Only under specific structural contexts, population growth and geography could help in the change of technology.

Marx considered that with the increase in population, common tribal property got reduced to small territorial units, giving further power to some of those selected few individuals who already had the privilege of safeguarding common interests and social functions. Under their leadership, warfare was carried out, usually for competition over resources.[23] This initially served population dispersal, boundary adjustment, and consolidated the power of the chiefs. Later, with further development of forces of production, wars were launched more to conquer slaves who could be made to pay tribute than to conquer waste lands.

Be that as it may, for Marx, class society appeared with the transition of consumption economy to a productive economy with regular surplus products for exchange. And this transition was possible with the development of productive forces and change from natural to social division of labour. In primitive society, there was only gift exchange of several types, which created and reinforced relationships of alliance between individuals and groups. It was with the advent of inter-tribal trade that there appeared individualization which was absent in the primitive men and even-

22. Martins Orans, 'Surplus,' *Human Organization*, No. 25, 1966.

23. Marvin Harris, *Cows, Pigs, Wars and Witches*, Knoff, New York, 1974.

tually classes became not only materially possible but mandatory for social order. Engels writes : "The appearance of private property in herds of cattle and articles of luxury led to exchange between individuals, to the transformation of products into *commodities*. Here lies the root of the entire revolution that followed."[24]

But this explanation is problematic for two reasons. Firstly, trade is a rather universal phenomenon. The archaeological and prehistoric information demonstrate that all societies, notwithstanding their level of development, had maintained certain amount of reciprocal transfer of production, because they were never entirely self-sufficient. This archaic trade loosely linked various primitive communities of different regions with different resources, and of different specialized occupations. This means certain goods were produced over and above the local needs, and that such a surplus production was felt necessary to meet certain needs of the group itself. Therefore primitive economy was not necessarily subsistence economy, and that inequal organized distribution of precious goods meant that the exchange were ultimately linked to the reproduction of the social relations of the primitive order itself.[25] The exchanges are of course conditioned by the form and patterning of the societies. In any case, trade, being historically universal, cannot be the cause of a historically specific phenomenon of class. It may either be concomitant or contingent. Nonetheless, if a qualitative distinction is conceptualized between archaic trade and advanced trade, then a causal relationship may be possible. Secondly, if in primitive society, the exchange is only cyclical, in the sense that wealth is consumed or redistributed or destroyed at death, then the inherent tendency would logically be against accumulation, and therefore, against the development of productive forces. As a result, there can neither be commodity production nor social division of labour.

Moreover, Marx's interest being largely focused on the rise of private property, a legal category of highly developed class society,

24. Marx Engels, *op. cit.*, p. 402.

25. Jean-Michel Servet, 'Primitive Order and Archaic Trade, *Economy and Society*, Vol. X, No. 4, pp. 423-46.

the insights into the total process of change remain incomplete. The totality. cannot be grasped only in terms of the ownership of property. And since the explanatory principle is derived from the analysis of capitalism, the position is further weak. These remarks do not amount to belitting the significance. The point is to develop it.

In primitive society, the major scarce resource was human labour, which was used collectively against nature to expropriate the product from it. In this process of dialectical interaction, both the forms of co-operation and nature itself got changed. For a very long time, this dialectics itself necessitated development of forces of production. But when further development of forces of production appeared impossible within the co-operation of labour, a change was needed in the nature of co-operation for further control and use of nature. Fortunately, a certain amount of surplus is already generated for internal and external exchange, which in turn created and reproduced a hierarchical structure of politico-religious personnel and others. Because of their specific functions in the community, the first stratum could tend to divorce from the process of direct production. But the members of that stratum could not reproduce themselves until the archaic trade got expanded and the warfare got structurally regularized. Then the members could live without adequately sharing the work while receiving a proportionately higher share of the products for exchange. Such a divorce of a few members from the process of production might facilitate the development of productive forces, which in turn, developed production, commodity exchange and division of labour, eventually leading to the formation of class society. In other words, more than property and exchange, the in-built mechanisms within labour co-operation for permitting certain people to live without labour ultimately changed the character of the co-operation of labour, and created conditions for the formation of class society. This is only schematic and much more serious thinking and substantiation is necessary before some definite laws of change of primitive society can be determined.

All the above explanations may partially or fully explain the natural dynamics of primitive societies. But since, at least the time of colonialism, the process is obtruded by the external colonial capital, it is a dialectical integration of two sets of productive systems. The dynamics of primitive societies of today, therefore, cannot be understood without a consideration of the articulation of the political economy of colonialism, capitalism and other class systems. This process is however much more complex than what is discussed in this paper. We hope to take up this at some other time.

# 11

# TOWARDS AN APPRAISAL OF HISTORICAL MATERIALISM

THE TRANSITION FROM one stage of production to another poses problems of the greatest importance for Marxist theory and political action. Until the beginning of nineteen-sixties, students of Marxism have generally propagated the view of dominance of the economic base and the dependence of the superstructure on the base, and assumed that the development of society is governed by implicable laws, and therefore, has a natural process of chronological succession of universal stages, inexorably leading to the process of realization of a communist society. This interpretation of historical materialism lavishly concentrated on the early writings of Marx and Engels, and was strongly critical towards any other interpretation of Marxism. Of course at that time Marxism was the 'monopoly' of the established communist parties of the world—dominated by the Soviet Communist Party. But the concrete accumulated experience of the world since the Chinese revolution in the late 1940s, reprobated the oversimplified evolutionary and teleological notion of the movement of history.

As a consequence of the difficulty of explaining the world event through the mechanistic determinism of history held by the communist parties, a rethinking of historical materialism was carried out by several eminent scholars. 'The development of underdevelopment school revolted against the orthodox interpretation of historical materialism and its emphasis on modes of production, and insisted the hierarchial unity' of the capitalist world in metropolis-satellite relations. This school conceived that the satellite countries can become socialist by armed national ilbe-ration struggles against international capital. But the view of the all-pervasive penetration of the capitalist world market and the universal absolute drain of surplus from the underdeveloped areas, appeared as another simple mechanistic generalization. Gradually, other flaws in this theoretical formulation are challenged.

The major disapproval of the orthodox interpretation of historical materialism came from the Althusserian school which emphasizing the later works of Marx and his recent publications, like *Grundrisse,* put forward an abstract structuralist interpretation of 'basis and superstructure' and the mode of their hierarchial interactions. But although the proponents of the school returned back to the question of mode of production, they have ignored the generality in history and the role of the subjective elements in social transformations.

Thus, in the course of a century since the *Communist Manifesto,* the nature and meaning of historical materialism have taken, at least, three diametrically opposed interpretations. In the confines of space available here, it is almost impossible to attempt any systematic evaluation of the total idea of Marx on historical materialism. Therefore, we limit ourselves to the evaluation of the popular interpretation of historical materialism and also the later developments in the field. Towards the end, we attempt a few concluding and a few inclusive remarks for an appraisal of historical materialism.

## I

Stages and motive forces of historical development have been the most controversial features of marxist historical theory. Till recently, the most of the Marxist scholars,[1] basing on the early

1. Particularly, G. V. Plekhanov, *Fundamental Problems of Marxism,* Progress Publishers, Moscow, 1977; N. Bukharin, *Historical Materialism,* Russell and Russell Inc., 1965; George Luckacs, *History and Class Consciousness,* The Merlin Press, London, 1971; Karl Korsch, *Marxism and Philosophy,* New Left Books, London, 1970; Herbert Marcuse, *Reason and Revolution,* Beacon Press, Boston. 1960 and Henri Lefvebre, *Dialectical Materialism,* Jonathan Cape, London, 1968. They insisted on the importance of Hegel in the formation of Marx's thought and strongly disapproved of the positivistic interpretation of Marxism.

works of Marx and Engels,[2] distinguished five dintinct socio-economic formations, namely, primitive-communal, slave, feudal, capitalist and communist, socialist being the first phase of communism. Each of the formations has its own appropriate productive forces, the corresponding relations of production, and the superstructure. The development of the socio-economic formations ascends from the lower to the higher one.

Interestingly, those who conceived historical materialism in a unilinear process of development of society in a predetermined course have frequently quoted the famous passage from the "preface" to *A Contribution to the Critique of Political Economy*, where Max in 1859 wrote : "In *broad outlines*, we can designate *the Asiatic*, the ancient, the feudal and the modern bourgeois methods of production as so many epochs in the progress of the economic formation of society."[3] To them, this passage reflected the universal conception of human history as a whole. Obviously, the mention of the "broad outlines" in the quote has been ignored. Likewise, "the Asiatic" mode of production has not only remained unacknowledged but is consciously omitted from the 'schema', which for Marx, as we will see, was an independent socio-economic formation. These and other like omissions and distortions were greatly responsible for the evolutionary and teleological conception of historical materialism, which at least implicity denied the importance of historical materialism as an analytical tool for understanding and changing the concrete historical phenomena, as are evident in particular societies.

For the first time Marx, in his 'preface' to *A Contribution to the Critique of Political Economy*, brings the non-European world into his frame of the stages of historical development and attaches no less importance to the Asiatic mode of production than to the

2. For instance, *The German Ideology* (1846), Progress Publishers, Moscow, 1960; *The Poverty of Philosophy* (1847), Foreign Languages Publishing House, Moscow, n.d.; *The Communist Manifesto* (1848), International Publishers, New York, 1948; *A Contribution to the Critique of Political Economy* (1859), Charles H. Kerr, Chicago, 1904.

3. Marx, *A Contribution to the Critique of Political Economy*, *op. cit.*, p. 13, Emphasis added.

other modes of production. Marx viewed the Asiatic society as a static and traditional one with dispersed peasantry and a paternalistic centralized government, and was devoid of any social class or stratum capable of initiating social change.[4] It was marked by the absence of private property in land,[5] and the common need of water for agriculture,[6] leading to the emergence of centralized government which was the primary owner of the surplus product created through the ground rent in the form of taxes.[7] The self-sustaining unity between agriculture and manufacture (handicrafts) within the villages helped them to be self-sufficient, self-contained and autonomous units, cut off from the outside world. The existing division of labour precluded the development of classes and had constantly reproduced itself in the same way, which ultimately served as the basis for the perpetuation of the archaic system, and was the mainstay of oriental despotism.[8] In the context of India, Marx noted that the annihilation of the traditional Asiatic society could be carried out by the diffusion of British influence which would eventually result in laying down the material foundations of capitalism in the country.[9]

4 Thus he writes : "Indian society has no history at all, at least no *known* history. What we call its history, is but the history of the successive intruders who founded their empires on the passive basis of that unresisting and unchanging society." Emphasis added. Marx, "The Future Results of the British Rule in India," in Marx and Engels, *On Colonialism*, Foreign Languages Publishing House, Moscow, n.d., p. 76. Emphasis added. The critics of Marx and Asiatic Society forget the use of 'known' in the passage.

5. Marx, 'Lord Canning's Proclamation and Land Tenure in India,' in *On Colonialism*, *op. cit.*, pp. 162-165.

6. Marx, 'The British Rule in India,' in *On Colonialism*, *op. cit.*, pp. 31-37.

7. David McLellan, *Marx's Grundrisse*, Paladin, London, 1973, pp. 132-134.

8. Engels, *Anti-Duhring*, Progress Publishers, Moscow, 1969, pp. 214-217, 366. See also Marx and Engels, *The German Ideology*, *op. cit.*, pp. 31-39 and L. Krader, *The Asiatic Mode of Production*, Van Gorcum, Assen, 1975 and *The Dialectic of Civil Society*, Van Gorcum, Assen, 1977.

9. Marx, 'The Future Results of the British Rule in India,' *op. cit.*, pp. 79 ff. About the three different influences of the conquering powers on the local mode of production, see Karl Marx, *Grundrisse : Foundations of the Critique of Political Economy*, Penguin Books, 1973, p. 97.

From the standpoint of unilinear theory of history, the concept of Asiatic mode contains problems of crucial importance to the structure of historical materialism. Firstly, though the Asiatic mode was not thought of as a geographical category—as it did not involve the whole of Asia—while including some parts of Africa (*e.g.* Egypt),[10] it no doubt referred to a specific formation,[11] mainly depending on the ecological conditions and artificial water supply.[12] Secondly, the notion that the Asiatic society has no history is by itself startling ; and the existence of state without social classes brought problems to the relationship between base and superstructure, particularly about the formation of state.[13] Lastly, the view of the society as an unchanging and passive one and its possible development through the impact of Western bourgeois society seems to be terribly, undialectical. Moreover, the assumption of the lack of internal mechanism and internal forces for the transformation of society is basically Hegelian.

Pointing to these criticisms, the Marxists, till recently, have ignored the significance of the concept of Asiatic mode and insisted on the succession of European social stages as universal. Thus, we are told that the Asiatic mode was nothing but a particular form of feudal mode.[14] But Marx nowhere interpreted likewise. On the other hand, even in 1879, he argued that India

10. An excellent account is given in Y. Varga, 'The Asiatic Mode of Production,' in *Politico-Economic Problems of Capitalism*, Progress Publishers, Moscow, 1968, pp. 330-351.

11. Engels mentions this in a letter to Marx, 6 June, 1853, Marx and Engels, *Selected Correspondence*, Progress Publishers, Moscow, 1965, pp. 82-83.

12. Some have even argued that since the materialist conception of history is applicable to mankind as a whole, introducing Asiatic mode would exclude analysis of the vast majority of people from the purview of historical materialism. See Duniel Thorner, 'Marx on India and the Asiatic Mode of Production,' in *Contribution to Indian Sociology*, vol. IX, 1966, pp. 60-63.

13. See, for instance, Berry Hindess and Paul Q. Hirst, *Pre-Capitalist Modes of Production*, Routledge and Kegan Paul, London, 1975.

14. For example, V. Pavlov, *Indian Capitalist Class: A Historical Study*, People's Publishing House, Delhi, 1964, p. 1.

was not feudal and on that basis he had criticised Kovalevsky.[15] Nonetheless, some continue to argue that the weakness in the information available to Marx during his early days made him to formulate the concept of Asiastic mode and later on with evidence he had neglected it.[16] This is a false conclusion indeed, for despite the discrepancy in his theoretical frame, he continued to assert and elaborate the asiatic mode in even in his last volume of *Capital*—where of course, with the availability of more material, he had somewhat changed his extremely critical view of stagnancy of the Asiatic societies.[17]

It is true that Marx had certain empirical defects on the nature of society, and so he overestimated both the destructive and constructive impact of colonialism on the "third world."[18] There can be amendments and developments on Marx's conception of stagnation of Asiatic society. These materials, however, are of specific nature, whereas introducing the concept of Asiatic mode into the framework has been stimulating a new heuristic approach to Marxist

15. For Marx the history of Asia and the categories for the compensation of it are not to be subsumed under the history of Europe and the European historical categories. E.J. Hobsbawm, 'Introduction,' in Marx, *Pre-Capitalist Economic Formations,* Lawrence and Wishart, London, 1964, p. 58. For details, see L.S. Gamayunov and R.A. Ulyanovsky, 'The Work of the Russian Sociologist M.M. Kovalevsky. . .and Marx's Criticism of the Work,' XXV International Congress of Orientalists. Oriental Literature Publishing House, Moscow, 1960, pp. 1-10 and Krader, *The Asiatic Mode of Production. op. cit.*, chapters 4 and 5.

16. Irfan Habib, 'Problems of Marxist Historical Analysis,' in K.M. Kurian (ed.), *India : State and Society*, Orient Longman, Bombay, 1975, p. 23 and 'An Examination of Wittfogel's Theory of Oriental Despotism,' in *Enquiry*, vol. 6, pp. 54-73. See also D. D. Kosambi's review of K. A. Wittfogel's *Oriental Despotism : A Comparative Study of Total Power* (Yale University Press, New Haven, 1957) in *Economic Weekly*, 2 November, 1957, p. 1717.

17. George Lichtheim, *The Concept of Ideology and Others Essays*, Vintage Books, New York, 1967, pp. 74-76. He, of course, notes his difficulty in locating Asiatic society. See also Hobsbawm, *op. cit.*, pp. 23-91, *passim*.

18. Eric Stokes 'The First Century of British Colonial Rule in India : Social Revolution or Social Stagnation,' in *Past and Present*, No. 58, 1973, pp. 136-160.

historiography,[19] and challenging the notion of linear and closed history which was thought to be governed by immutable universal laws leading to a single goal.

We have taken the liberty of presenting this lengthy observation on Asiatic society because it goes to the heart of the question of Marx's conception of movement of history and challenges the orthodox interpretation of historical materialism.

Besides the Asiatic mode of production, the publication of Marx's *Grundrisse* (1857-58)[20] and other little known works of Marx and Engels reprobated the orthodoxy of unilinear conception of history. These lately published works serve as a powerful reminder that Marx was not the seller of ready-made truths for all societies and all times, instead he was simply a maker of tools to study the societies in their concrete situations of existence and dynamics. In *Grundrisse*, Marx saw the issue of stages of historical development as highly complex and observed that societies need not necessarily pass through all the epochs. He himself during his lifetime continued to add new dimensions to the pre-capitalist social formations in the light of his increasing historical knowledge, from time to time. Evidently, though both Marx and Engels took much interest in the Asiatic mode of production and the early history of German and Slavonic tribes, their analysis was deliberately tentative and inconclusive, merely indicating the possible trends in the specific situations.[21] This shows their awareness of the weakness of their information on pre-capitalist societies, and hence unlike the "Marxists"; they did not had any ready-made scheme.

Marx and Engels were strongly critical of explaining historical

19. For example, Hobsbawm, *op. cit.*; B. McFurlane and S. Cooper, 'The Asiatic Mode of Production,' in *Australian Quarterly*, vol. 38, No. 3, September 1966, pp. 27-43; V. Kiernan, Marx and India', in Miliband and Saville (eds.), *The Socialist Register 1967*. The Merlin Press, London, pp. 159-189 and also Ernest Mandel. *The Formation of the Economic Thought of Karl Marx*, New Left Books, London, 1971, p. 125.

20. Marx, *Grundrisse, op. cit.*, and also Hobsbawm, *op. cit.*

21. See particularly L. Krader, *The Ethnological Notebooks of Karl Marx*, Van Gorcum, Assen, 1972. This is a very useful document for Marxist anthropology.

processes solely in terms of the general types of socio-economic formations.[22] To them, mode of production was an abstract category and can never be found in a pure form. In most historically constituted communities, the production relations do not in their totality conform to a single type with a homogeneous structure. For instance, there is not a single illustration in human history, where the whole working population was enslaved. Instead, in every slave society, there were survivals of primitive communism, the rising traces of feudalism, existence of independent petty-producers, and also in many cases, an emerging merchant class. Likewise, there is no perfect example of feudal system.[23] Capitalism and socialism too have never existed in their full pristine glory, reality is always an admixture of more than one mode of production.

It follows then that in almost every society, besides a predominant mode of production, there exists one or more other forms. Marx was quite aware of hisorical specific socio-economic formations under the decisive frame of a single dominant mode of production. Thus, he rightly said that over the same economic basis, there may be endless variations and gradations due to innumerable empirical circumstances, natural environment, racial composition effects of eternal historical influences, and so on, and can be understood only through the analysis of these empirically given conditions.[24] This is clearly demonstrated by the way he deals with the different forms of capital itself. He observed that even in a fully developed capitalist society, the earlier forms of capital—interest-bearing and merchant — perform definite functions and participate in the distribution of surplus value.[25] Elsewhere, he

22. Marx, in fact, divided history into a number of different typologies of historical stages at various points in his work mainly depending on his historical knowledge and as aids to his analysis of specific problems. See Shlomo Avineri, 'Introduction,' in *Karl Marx on Colonialism and Modernization*, Anchor Books, New York, 1969, pp. 1-31.

23. Engels, letter to Schmidt, 12 March, 1958, *Selected Correspondence*, *op. cit.*, p. 484.

24. Marx, *Capital*, Progress Publishers, Moscow, 1971, vol. III, pp. 791-92, 885-87 and also *Capital*, vol. I, pp. 702-12.

25. *Ibid.*, vol. III, parts IV and V.

maintained that the remnants of vanishing social formations can even develop explicit significance within the progressive modes of production.[26] Besides, Marx also noted the existence of some sub-categories in the pre-capitalist formations such as Slavonic, which is a combination of elements from the Asiatic and feudal forms. At the same time, Lenin analysing the specific historical forms in the transition from feudalism to capitalism observed that the transitional society—semi-feudal—is an intrinsic form of the present.[27] In fact, Engels in a letter to Marx had actually spoken of the Ottoman empire as semi-feudal.[28] In periods of actual transition, it is even likely that a society may not be governed by any single mode of production.[29]

But Marx and Engels thought that these multiple forms of development in the pre-capitalist systems would cease with the increasing universalizing tendencies of capitalism.[30] They argued that the more developed the capitalist mode of production the less it would be adulterated and amalgamated with the survivals of earlier economic fomations.[31] Lenin, however, found in the early post-revolutionary Soviet Russia, a number of economic structures co-existing at a time.[32] The multi-structural social systems, where

26. Marx, *Grundrisse, op. cit.*, p. 105.

27. Lenin, 'The Development of Capitalism in Russia,' Chapters II-IV, *Collected Works*, Moscow, vol. 3, and also Mao Tse-tung, 'Analysis of the Classes in Chinese Society,' in his *Selected Works*, People Publishing House, Bombay, 1954, vol. I, pp. 13-21.

28. Engels' Letter to Marx, 22 December, 1882, Marx and Engels, *Selected Correspondence : 1846-1895*, National Book Agency, Calcutta, 1945, p. 363.

29. See Wlodzimier Wesolowski, 'Marx's Theory of Class Domination,' in Nicholas Lobkowicz (ed.) *Marx and the Western World*, the University Press, Notre Dame, 1967, p. 59.

30. For a description of the implications of Marx's view of universalizing nature of capitalism, see Shlomo, Avineri, *The Social and Political Thought of Karl Marx*, Cambridge University Press, 1968, pp. 150-174.

31. Marx, *Capital, op. cit.*, vol. III, p. 172.

32. Lenin in 1921 noted that at least there were five economic structures in the then Russia, namely, patriarchal economy, small commodity production, capitalist production, state capitalism and socialism. See his 'Report on the Tax in Kind,' *Collected Works, op. cit.*, vol. 32, pp. 295-296.

each structure constitutes a distinctive type of production relations with its specific laws of development, provide complex forms with greater class diversity. The simultaneous existence of various economic structures is not necessarily a transient phenomenon. They are often relatively stable and proceed very slowly. The mechanism of dialectical interaction between different structures is thus very complicated and beyond the comprehension of any mechanical scheme. In their own right they demand a detailed analysis to understand the trends of society, the motive forces of transformations and the relationship between the base and superstructure. Such multiplicity of economic systems are very common in most of the present day "third world" countries.

Apart from the coexistence of multiple structures and independent socio-economic formations in combination with the attributes of different modes of production, outside the five broad types, the founders of Marxism have also noted that the societies in their development may pass through different phases of disintegration depending upon their historical and social conditions. For instance, in the *Grundrisse*, Marx observed that there were three major alternative forms of development from primitive communal stage—Asiatic, feudal and ancient (slave based)—determined by the variations in the ecological, historical and ethnographical environment. Similarly, both Marx and Engels conceived that after the abolition of capitalism in the West, the backward countries can become socialist, without going through the capitalist stage.[33] With reference to Russia they suggested that the Russian peasantry may directly move from the feudal to the socialist stage.

Further, contrary to the orthodox Marxist faith, Marx had neither regarded that communism was itself 'the aim of human development or the final form of human society,'[34] nor ever claimed the discovery of predestined stages through which all societies must pass. He also did not consider progress as continuous and

33. Marx and Engels, *Selected Works*, Progress Publishers, Moscow, 1970, vol. III, pp. 480-81.

34. T. B. Bottomore and M. Rubel (eds.), *Karl Marx : Selected Writings in Sociology and Social Philosophy*, Penguin Books, 1974, p. 252.

inevitable and without any occasional regression. A society in unstable disequilibrium can theoretically move equally well forward or backward. Objecting to the oversimplified notion of progress, Lenin once said "... It is undialectical, unscientific and theoretically wrong to regard the course of world history as smooth and always in a forward direction, without occasional gigantic leaps back."[35]

In sum, the Asiatic society, multi-structural system, indpendent sub-categories and transitional forms outside the five general stages of human history, multilinear development of pre-capitalist societies, the view of communism as not being an end in itself and the occasional backward leaps of history together prove that Marx had strongly disavowed a unilinear theory of historical progression and did not insist that all societies have to pass the same stages without deviations, breaks in continuity and reverses. The interpreters of Marx have however, in the name of Marxism introduced an evolutionary and teleological conception of human history into the realm of historical materialism. Nevertheless, Marx's conception of multilinear development in the pre-capitalist societies, and unilinear development with the development of capitalism due to its universalizing tendencies, has become an area of academic disputes since the beginning of 1960s. The forthcoming section would deal with this problem in detail.

## II

On the basis of the above mentioned evidence against the conception of unilinear progression of human society and the concrete world experience, particularly after the Chinese revolution in the late 1940s, a theory of "development and dependency" has been forwarded in the beginning of the 1960s, which strongly attacked the conception of historical materialism and its emphasis on modes of production. Prior to this theory, Mao Tse-tung from his revolutionary experience had already challenged the orthodox

35. Lenin, 'The Junius Pamphlet,' *Collected Works*, *op. cit.*, vol. 22, p. 310.

line by developing a model in 1940, which conceived that imperialism would not permit the establishment of a capitalist society in China under the bourgeois dictatorship,[36] and the peasants and workers through an armed revolution against feudalism and international capital simultaneously would transform China into a socialist state.[37] Success of the socialist revolution in semi-feudal and semi-colonial China provided a striking impetus to the communist movement in the "third world" countries. The armed guerrilla tactics and the importance of peasantry as a revolutionary force influenced the leadership of the peasants' and workers' struggles in Cuba, the Philippines, Korea, Malaya and Indochina.

Besides this contribution to historical materialism, Mao has also argued that by itself the theory of productive forces is inadequate, and that the road to socialism must be led by ideological struggles rather than through production maximization. And further he said that ideas can also become a material force in a socialist society.[38] By these propositions the superstructure was given a new significance. But notwithstanding these contributions, Mao had retained the basic theoretical framework of historical materialism, the concept of modes of production and the importance of the leadership of the proletariat in the course of socialist transformation.

Now, in the 1960s, there were revolutionary upsurges throughout the "third world"—three insurgencies in Thailand, the Naxalite movement in India, the second Indochina war, revolutions in Angola, Mozambique, Rhodesia, Chand and other African countries, movements in Mexico, Argentina, Bolivia, Brazil, Uruguay and other Latin American countries. These

36. Mao Tse-tung, 'On New Democracy,' in his *Selected Works*, *op. cit.*, vol. III, pp. 106-156. See also Regis Debray, 'Problems of Revolutionary Strategy in Latin America,' in *New Left Review*, No. 45, September-October 1967, where he argued that development of capitalism is impossible within the orbit of world capitalism.

37. Mao Tse-tung, 'The Chinese Revolution and the Chinese Communist Party,' in his *Selected Works*, *op. cit.*, vol. III, pp. 72-101.

38. Joan Robinson, *The Cultural Revolution in China*, Penguin Books, 1970, p. 12.

struggles made a definite attack on the view of linearity of historical succession—which was propagated by the established communist parties of the world, particularly the pro-Moscow ones. In this context, the theory of development of underdevelopment was forwarded by A. Gunder Frank[39] and for sometime it could draw a considerable attention from many Marxists throughout the world, who were finding problems to understand the empirical reality within the orthodox historical framework.[40]

Frank, being influenced by Baran's notion of the roots of the backwardness[41] and the Cuban revolution,[42] focussed his attention on historical structural analysis of surplus extraction and tranfer, and structural subordination of periphery-economies through the local subordinate bourgeoisie. There was no consideration of relations of production and class conflicts developing within these.[43] For instance, with reference to Brazil, Frank spoke of "the myth of feudalism" and insisted that it is a part of the world capitalist system and thus could not be defined as a mode of production. The view of all-pervasive penetration of the capitalist world market, creating worldwide hierarchial unity of the capitalist system, offered the image of unified system with a centre and a

39. Andre Gunder Frank, *Capitalism and Underdevelopment in Latin America : Historical Studies of Chile and Brazil*, Monthly Review Press, New York, 1969, especially chapter IV.

40. For example, A. Emmanuel, *Unequal Exchange*, Monthly Review Press, 1972; S. Amin, *Accumulation on a World Scale*, Monthly Review Press, New York, 1974 and I. Wallerstein, 'The Rise and Future Demise of the World Capitalist System : Concepts for Comparative Analysis,' in *Comparative Studies in Society and History*, vol. 16, No. 4, 1974.

41. Paul A. Baran, *The Political Economy of Growth*, Monthly Review Press, New York, 1957 and also Baran and P. M. Sweezy, *Monopoly Capital : An Essay on the American Economic and Social Order*, Monthly Review Press, New York, 1966.

42. See Ted Wheelright, *Radical Political Economy : Collected Essays*, A. N. Z. Sydney, 1974, pp. 249-250.

43. But in one of his recent articles he talks about "the diversity of modes of production in the new world," which is definitely a development over his blanket view of capitalism. See his 'Development and Underdevelopment in the New World : Smith and Marx vs. the Weberians,' in *Theory and Society*, vol. 2, No. 4, Winter 1975.

periphery, or with hierarchial metropolis-satellite relations. Through this simplistic view, the interpretation of Mao that imperialism would not allow capitalism to grow in colonial and semi-colonial countries and that it is an ally to the pre-capitalist social formations was neglected, while the dependence theorists justified their position by quoting Marx who assumed that the universalizing tendencies of capitalism would ultimately unite the world. Marx's proposition was taken to the extreme without enough concrete evidence and the consideration of the character of imperialism.

Anyway, according to the formulation of world unity in a hierarchial relations, the concerned theorists have found only one general contradiction in the world and that is between the metropole bourgeoisie and the masses of the periphery.[44] Frank, alike, Baran and Sweezy,[45] thus argued that the centre of socialist revolution is in the "third world" and in order to build socialist society within an independent "third world" country, there should be armed national liberation struggles against international capital at all levels.[46]

This theory, after receiving an initial spontaneous appeal in the" third world" was brought under scrutiny and its flaws were explored. The notion of assimilated colonial and semi-colonial societies into a world-wide capitalist system in a subordinate position has been challenged from the point of view of mode of production.[47] The emphasis upon the extraction of surplus and its essential investment in the metropoles has neglected the conditions under which the production of surplus takes place.[48] It does

44. See James Petras, 'New Perspectives on Imperialism and Social Classes in Periphery,' in *Journal of Contemporary Asia*, vol. 5, No. 3, 1975.

45. Baran and Sweezy, *op.cit.*

46. Frank, *op. cit.*, p. 344 and also his 'Dependance is Dead—Long Live Dependence and the Class struggle : An Answer to Critics,' in *Latin American Perspectives*, Vol. I, No. 1, 1974. In this eassay he admits that he is not a Marxist.

47. Largely the criticism came from the neo-structuralists who have taken for granted that Frank is a Marxist. See Ernesto Laclau, 'Imperialism in Latin America,' in *New Left Review*, No. 67, May-June 1971.

48. See P. J. O'Brien, 'A Critique of Latin American Theories of Dependency,' in I. Oxaal, T. Barnett and D. Booth (eds.), *Beyond the Sociology of Development*, London, 1975.

not say why the "third world" was not developed in the past and why not now it becomes developed with its cheap labour and raw material. Besides, the concept of development does not distinguish between the USA and Portugal, and the concept of underdevelopment between India and Tanzania. It is indeed an arbitrary division.

In short, the theory offers only a general, simplistic interpretation of trade between developed and underdeveloped countries and fails to give any insight into the production relations. Further, the assumption of the world-wide unity of capitalism and the unevenness of its development ignores the question of historical and structural particularities in the different countries, especially in the "third world" which would ultimately determine their developments.

## III

In the late 1960s, the influence of the theory of "development and dependency" was considerably eroded by the critics belonging to the neo-structuralist school. In contrast to Frank, they re-emphasized the forces and relations of production, the Marxist value theory and capital accumulation and crisis, and strongly criticised the Baran-Sweezy-Frank school for their overlooking of these aspects. At the same time, the theory of chronological succession of definite stages has also been equally rebuked and disapproved by the neo-structuralist school by stressing the importance of analytically ranking the socio-economic formations.

Before analysing the sophisticated theoretical and philosophical structure of the neo-structuralist school, it appears necessary to mention about the structuralism of Levi-Strauss, whose influence on this school is significant. Levi-Strauss insisted that the elements and developments of a social phenomenon acquire meaning only as aspects of a definite totality as elements of a specific system, and hence the analysis of the structures of social phenomenon is the *sine quo non* for understanding society.[49] Historical materialism

49. C. Levi-Strauss, *Structural Anthropology*, Allen Lane, The Penguin Press, London, 1968 and also his 'The Structural Study of Myth' in *Journal of American Folklore*, vol. 68, No. 270, 1955.

does not deny the significance of examining the different social structures and their components in their unity and diversity. But he goes further. For instance, he speaks of kinship systems (other social institutions too) as a "co-ordinated ensemble, the function of which is to ensure the permanency of the social group."[50] While arguing for discovering the basic and universal structural elements of all human societies,[51] he assumes that since all cultures are the product of human brains, there must be common universal features somewhere beneath the surface, at the level of structure which one can never notice at the level of manifest fact.[52] The concealment is due to the nature of the structure itself and has nothing to do with the level of consciousness.[53] This is an extremely reductionist position and the approach is intentionally anti-historical. Social realities are historically specific and are not general as assumed by Levi-Strauss. The model evading history fails to locate the determinants of the diverse forms of social structure and is divorced far away from explaining the social transformations from one structure to another.

The neo-structuralist school of Althusser and his associates hold that the concept of mode of production is an abstract object referring to a matrix of structures, institutions and relationships. The abstract matrix comprises of multiple internal structure—economic, ideological and juridico-political—and their interaction between one another, wherein economic relations, *in the last analysis*, explain the relations of the entire structure.[54] Thus the social

50. See Sal Tax *et al* (eds.), *An Appraisal of Anthropology Today*, Chicago, 1962, p. 343 and also Levi-Strauss, *The Elementary Structures of Kinship*, Eyre & Spottiswoode, London, 1969.

51. Levi-Strauss, *The Savage Mind*, Weidenfeld Nicolson, London, 1966, concluding chapter.

52. For a discussion, see E. Leach, *Levi-Strauss*, Fontana, London, 1970, pp. 21-36; D. Robey (ed.), *Structuralism : An Inrtoduction*, Clarendon Press, Oxford, 1973 and M. Lane (ed.), *Structuralism : A Reader*, Jonathan Cape, London, 1970.

53. Levi-Strauss, 'On Structure,' in his *Structural Anthropolagy*, *op. cit.*, p. 279.

54. See L. Althusser and E. Balibar, *Reading Capital*, New Left Books, London, 1970.

formations are only the concrete forms observable in historical societies.[55] These formations are naturally innumerable while the concept of 'modes' being ideal and analytical categories are few.[56] These forms can be understood from an *a priori* valid axiom of modes of production which must be empirically verified in each case. The relations which do not fit in with the theoretical model is explained as due to the coexistence of different modes within any concrete social formation where, of course, it is presumed that *one of the modes* dominates the social formation.[57]

Althusser argued that there are multiplicity of contradictions existing at all levels of the social formation, and each one has its own 'history' with complex interactions. Hence determination is never simple. It is always complex and multiple.[58] To recognize this complexity, he says, is to give greater precision to the relationship between various social levels.[59] This has appealed to anthropologists in their search for dominant social relations or mode of production besides kinship governing the primitive and peasant societies.[60]

55. For instance, N. Poulantzas, *Political Power and Social Classes*, New Left Books, London, 1973. For a critique, see A. Wolfe, 'New Directions in the Marxist Theory of Politics,' in *Politics and Society*, vol. 4, No. 2. 1974.

56. For a discussion, see Paresh Chattopadhyay, 'On the Question of Mode of Production in Indian Agriculture,' in *Economic and Political Weekly* (Review of Agriculture), March 25, 1972, Section I.

57. L. Althusser, *For Marx*, New Left Books, London, 1971 and Lucio Colletti, *From Rousseau to Lenin*, New Left Books, London, 1972.

58. For this suggestion, see Althusser and Balibar, *op. cit.*, p. 153.

59. *Ibid.*

60. For instance, Maurice Godelier 'Structure and Contradiction in *Capital*,' in Robin Blackburn (ed.), *Ideology in Social Science : Readings in Critical Social Theory*, Fontana, London, 1972, pp. 334-368 and his article in Maurice Bloch (ed.), *Marxist Analysis and Social Anthropology*, Vol. II, Malaby Press, London, 1975; Emmanuel Terray, *Marxism and "Primitive" Societies : Two Studies*, Monthly Review Press, New York, 1972; Claude Meillassoux, 'From Reproduction to Production,' in *Economy and Society*, Vol. I, No. 1, February 1972, pp. 93-105 and his (edited) *The Development of Trade and Markets in West Africa*, Oxford University Press, London, 1971. It may be mentioned here that Levi-Strauss once observed that the low level of

Today, of course, all varieties of 'Marxists' agree that in addition to the predominant mode which approximates the reality, the other modes need specific investigations in their own right. With regard to the question of determination, Althusser also speaks of economic structure determining the social formation, in the last instance. He too did not say what he meant by the last instance and did not attempt to explore what determines what and under what circumstances. In this sense, the major, structural problem of historical materialism continues to be unsolved.

About the assumption that the understanding of the social structure is necessary to analyse the progress of society, there is no dispute. Marx always held this. He said: "It is always the direct relationship of the owners of the conditions of production to the direct producers . . . which reveals the innermost secret, the hidden basis of the entire social structure."[61] But in the process, the neo-structuralists, while working with elements in permutations and combinations to explain the concrete reality, denied the theory of historical transition based on different class struggles in different societies. Althusser, for example, argues that the phenomena of genesis and transformation can automatically be deduced from the basic structure of a given social formation. By this, the two basic elements of historical materialism—consciousness and action—are completely eliminated. The neo-structuralist school claims that scientific Marxism contains not men and men's action, but the social structures and social formations that invisibly move them and shape history.[62]

With some obscure analysis, Althusser says that Marx was basically a structuralist and considered historical analysis as only

development of the structure of the production forces in the primitive societies imposes co-operation and group life for subsistance and reproduction, which ultimately gives the complex structure and dominant role of kinship relations. See his *Structural Anthropology*, *op. cit.*, p. 48.

61. Marx, *Capital*, Progress Publishers, Moscow, 1959, Vol. III, p. 772.

62. Althusser and Balibar, *op. cit.*, p. 112. For criticism of this point of view, see Mirian Glucksmann, *Structuralist Analysis in Contemporary Social Thought*, Routledge and Kegan Paul, London, 1974, pp. 137, 173.

secondary to structural.[63] To support this position he and his associates have stressed on the later works of Marx and criticised the earlier works which give emphasis on the liberating potential of class struggle. Their stress on the later works is guided by their motive for holding the maxim that structures of society and their contradictions determine social outcome.[64]

But it is improper to argue that Marxism gives only secondary importance to history. In fact, as we will see in the coming section, that Marxism considers that towards understanding society both historical and structural analyses are indispensable, inseparable and complementary to each other. Marx was concerned both with the question of periods of human history and with their negations. In short, neo-structuralism with its complete neglect of class struggles, the role played by men in the movement of history and the historical development provides only unintelligible model of internal contradictions in social phenomena.

## IV

In the foregoing we have noticed three distinct ways of interpretation of historical materialism. The schematic view of movement of history in a chronological order was propagated by the pro-Moscow Communist Parties of the world, and that interpretation of historical materialism had dominated for a pretty long time. But the socialist revolutionary struggles in pre-capitalist societies since the late 1940s posed problem to the popular orthodox interpretation of historical materialism. As a product of that in the beginning of the 1960s a few Marxist intellectuals, largely concerned with Latin American countries, extended a theory of "development and dependency," which holds that the

63. Althusser, *op.cit.* For criticism of this position, Leszek Kolakowski, 'Althusser's Marx,' in Miliband and Saville (eds.) *The Socialist Register 1971*. The Merlin Press, London, pp. 111-28, and for presentation, see Maurice Godelier, 'System Structure and Contradiction in *'Capital,'* in *The Socialist Register 1967*, The Merlin Press, London, pp. 91-119.

64. See, for instance, Albert Wellmer, *Critical Theory of Society*, Herder and Herder, New York, 1971.

world is united in a hierarchical order due to the development of capitalism in Europe and Northern America. This theory, in a sense, rejected the fundamental premises of historical materialism and its emphasis on modes of production. In contrast, the French Marxist philosopher Althusser and his associates have returned back to the question of modes of production and provided a neo-structuralist interpretation of society. Their analytical ranking of different levels in a society, particularly capitalistic, neglected the importance of history and the role of class consciousness in the process of social transformation. This approach too diluted the essence of historical materialism.

These diverse positions have produced enough academic and political confusion, and once more suggest that a large part of the difficulty lies with the absence of bringing out a correct connexion between theory and political practice of the oppressed masses. Historical materialism is not a mere academic knowledge for its own sake but knowledge to be used by Man in changing the world, which in turn, is the essential condition for the development of science of knowledge However, being conscious of this, let us trace the major sources of weakness of these contradictory formulations.

With regard to the view of universal unilinear succession of society, the founders had repeatedly emphasized that each society can be understood and ordered in terms of concrete analysis of situations, which comprise the material forces of production, the social relations of production and reproduction. They have never given any ready made scheme ; and only provided a materialist theory and methodology which can be used in different concrete historical formations. There is a living link between the theory and methodology. The unity is inseparable in any scientific study. Their abstract model is an analytical device intended to be only an approximate representation of historical reality. The predictions are carried out by extrapolating the laws and tendencies into the future. In short, historical materialism provides the method for analysing concrete history through the unity of general principles and specific situations, in their interconnexion and movement. A neglect of the dialectics between the universal and the particular appears to be the major weakness of the early interpretors of historical materialism.

The development of underdevelopment theory by its blanket generalization of the unity of world has overemphasized Marx's notion of universalizing capacity of capitalism without enough concrete historical and structural analysis. From the historical materialist point of view, this theory is of very limited significance.

The last variety has two major weaknesses arising out of the stress on structure and objectivity to the near complete neglect of general historical dynamics and the role of subjective elements. This is because of the structuralist methodology and its primary focus on only one mode of production—capitalism. Unlike the first type, here generality is almost totally rejected and particularity is absolutized. Emphasis is given only to dialectical method. Divorced from theory, method has lost its real content and turned into arbitrary juggling with categories and concepts which utimately may become an instrument of voluntarism and subjectivism. The general is neither a collection of petrified canons nor a dried mummy. It develops with experience and social practice which are constantly changing. Though cognition of the essence of the general is insufficient, it is essential for understanding the concrete. The facts themselves are of limited importance; only the link between the universal and the specific which provides the inner objective logic, is important.

Likewise the total rejection of subjective elements in the process of social transformation is obviously biased and unfounded. For Marx, history was a dialectical unity of three inseparable things : the development in accordance with the objective laws, primarily economic; the corresponding development of consciousness; and corresponding action expressed in the form of class struggles leading to revolutionary transformations of social formations. No doubt, Marx emphasized the objective economic conditions for a successful revolution, but did not reject the subjective elements, as propagated by the Althusserian school. The practical revolutionaries, like Lenin, Mao, Castro, Guevara and others, in their practice realized the importance of subjective factors like correct theories, political activities, party organization and ideological commitments, and thereby brought a synthesis between objective and subjective factors. A social revolution demands unity of objective and subjective conditions.

In sum, the roots of the differences in the three approaches lie in their overemphasis on one or the other elements of historical materialism, namely, the history vs. structure, the universal vs. particular, and the subjective vs. the objective. A scientific analysis of the dialectical unity of these elements can only explore the essence of historical materialism, and not simple insistence on a set of elements or the other.

# INDEX